The Rational Guide To

SQL Server 2005
Service
Broker

PUBLISHED BY

Rational Press - An imprint of the Mann Publishing Group
710 Main Street, 6th Floor
PO Box 580
Rollinsford, NH 03869, USA
www.rationalpress.com
www.mannpublishing.com
+1 (603) 601-0325

ISBN: 1-932577-27-0
Library of Congress Control Number (LCCN): 2006923186
Printed and bound in the United States of America.
10 9 8 7 6 5 4 3 2

Trademarks

Mann Publishing, Mann Publishing Group, Agility Press, Rational Press, Inc.Press, NetImpress, Farmhouse Press, BookMann Press, The Rational Guide To, Rational Guides, ExecuGuide, AdminExpert, From the Source, the Mann Publishing Group logo, the Agility Press logo, the Rational Press logo, the Inc.Press logo, Timely Business Books, Rational Guides for a Fast-Paced World, and Custom Corporate Publications are all trademarks or registered trademarks of Mann Publishing Incorporated.

All brand names, product names, and technologies presented in this book are trademarks or registered trademarks of their respective holders.

Disclaimer of Warranty

While the publisher and author(s) have taken care to ensure accuracy of the contents of this book, they make no representation or warranties with respect to the accuracy or completeness of the contents of this book and specifically disclaim any implied warranties or merchantability or fitness for a specific purpose. The advice, strategies, or steps contained herein may not be suitable for your situation. You should consult with a professional where appropriate before utilizing the advice, strategies, or steps contained herein. Neither the publisher nor author(s) shall be liable for any loss of profit or any other commercial damages, including but not limited to special, incidental, consequential, or other damages.

Credits

Author:	Roger Wolter
Technical Editor:	Dirk Myers
Editorial Director:	Jeff Edman
Book Layout:	Molly Barnaby
Series Concept:	Anthony T. Mann
Cover Concept:	Marcelo Paiva

All Mann Publishing Group books may be purchased at bulk discounts.

The Rational Guide To

SQL Server 2005
Service
Broker

Roger Wolter
Program Manager
SQL Server Service Broker
Microsoft Corporation

RATIONAL
PRESS

An imprint of the
www.mannpublishing.com

About the Author

Roger Wolter has 29 years of experience in various aspects of the computer industry, including jobs at Unisys, Infospan, Fourth Shift, and the last seven years as a Program Manager at Microsoft. His projects at Microsoft include COM+, SQLXML, the Soap Toolkit, SQL Server Service Broker, and SQL Server Express. His interest in Service Broker was sparked by a messaging-based manufacturing system he worked on in a previous life. He's currently splitting his time between the Service Broker and SQL Server Express projects in SQL Server 2005.

Acknowledgements

I started this project because I wanted to write the first Service Broker book on the market. I thought I was in trouble when John Grisham released *The Broker*, but it turns out that wasn't about the same Broker.

I would like to thank my wife Connie and my kids Erin, Kristen, and Erica for their support and encouragement. I couldn't have written this book without help from the fathers of Service Broker: Gerald Hinson, Gus Hill and Pat Helland. Dirk Myers tech edited the whole book and Remus Rusanu—the evil tech reviewer—gave me a lot of help with the protocol and security sections. My editor Jeff Edman patiently translated my geek prose into real English and Tony Mann gave me help and encouragement throughout the whole process. Jan Shanahan helped me get started and find a publisher. Bob Beauchemin and Dan Sullivan reviewed the book and gave me a lot of useful feedback.

Most of all, I would like to thank the whole Service Broker team: Gerald, Gus, Pat, Ivan, Al, Mike, Rushi, Marius, Raghu, Srini, Annamalai, Scott, Pete, Frank, Yumay, Jeff, Mihail, Carl, Xiaowei, Matt—and anyone else I forgot—for building a great product to write about.

About Rational Guides

Rational Guides, from Rational Press, provide a no-nonsense approach to publishing based on both a practicality and price that make them rational. Rational Guides are compact books of fewer than 224 pages. Each Rational Guide is constructed with the highest quality writing and production materials—at an affordable price. All Rational Guides are intended to be as complete as possible within the 224-page size constraint. Furthermore, all Rational Guides come with bonus materials, such as additional chapters, applications, code, utilities, or other resources. To download these materials, just register your book at www.rationalpress.com. See the instruction page at the end of this book to find out how to register your book.

Who Should Read This Book

This book is a valuable resource for both database programmers who want to write Service Broker applications and database administrators who have to support Service Broker applications. The reader does not need a background in Service Broker, but should have a basic knowledge of SQL Server and TSQL syntax. While previous Service Broker knowledge is not required to understand this book, much of the information will be useful to an intermediate Service Broker programmer or DBA.

To duplicate the samples in this book, the reader must have access to SQL Server 2005. Many of the examples can be done with the Express edition of SQL Server 2005, but the remote communications examples will require at least one licensed copy of SQL Server 2005.

Conventions Used In This Book

The following conventions are used throughout this book:

▶ *Italics* — First introduction of a term.

▶ **Bold** — Exact name of an item or object that appears on the computer screen, such as menus, buttons, dropdown lists, or links.

▶ `Mono-spaced text` — Used to show a Web URL address, computer language code, or expressions as you must exactly type them.

▶ **Menu1⇨Menu2** — Hierarchical Windows menus in the order you must select them.

Tech Tip:
This box gives you additional technical advice about the option, procedure, or step being explained in the chapter.

Note:
This box gives you additional information to keep in mind as you read.

Bonus:
This box lists additional free materials or content available on the Web after you register your book at `www.rationalpress.com`.

Caution
This box alerts you to special considerations or additional advice.

Contents

Contents

Contents

Contents

Service Broker Basics

Chapter 1

What is Service Broker?

One of the main goals for Microsoft SQL Server 2005 was to provide improved support for developing sophisticated database applications. The best known result of this emphasis was the integration of the .NET common language runtime into the database engine, but the XML Datatype and Service Broker are also significant additions to the database development environment. Taken together, these features enable a new class of database applications that perform significant processing in or close to the database. Service Broker provides the asynchronous infrastructure to build reliable, distributed database applications.

One example of an application that will benefit from Service Broker technology is a classic Web-based order entry application. When the Web user places an order, the application performs the minimum amount of work required to record the order in the database and go on to handle the next order. The back-office tasks required to fill the order—allocating inventory, shipping, billing, purchasing, etc.—are done asynchronously on separate servers, so that they don't impact the performance of the front-end application. Service Broker will reliably and transactionally manage these back-office functions to ensure that they will all be executed, even though the order entry application has moved on to handle other orders.

This book explains what Service Broker is and how it can be used to build reliable, distributed service-oriented applications. It is not intended to be a replacement for SQL Server Books Online, but rather a supplement that helps you understand why Service Broker works the way it does. To get the full benefit from this book, you should read SQL Server Books Online as well.

The first section of this book covers the new database objects that Service Broker uses to support asynchronous operations. The core concept of Service Broker applications is the *conversation*, covered in Chapter 2. Chapter 3 explains conversation groups, which solve many issues that multi-threaded messaging applications encounter. Chapter 4 introduces Service Broker queues and Chapter 5 describes the rest of the metadata used in the Service Broker infrastructure.

Part II introduces the Service Broker programming model. In Chapter 6, we learn about sending and receiving data using the Service Broker extensions to TSQL. Chapters 7, 8, and 9 explain more advanced topics in writing Service Broker applications.

Part III shows you how to extend your Service Broker application to communicate securely between distributed systems. Chapter 10 explains how to use routes to configure a distributed application and Chapter 11 presents the multi-layered Service Broker security system.

Part IV discusses some possible uses for Service Broker technology and covers the architectural issues that must be considered in Service Broker application design. A bonus chapter on troubleshooting and administration is available after you register your book online at www.rationalpress.com. See the instruction page at the end of this book to learn how to register.

Service Broker Architecture

Service Broker enables a new class of asynchronous, distributed database applications by offering unprecedented levels of reliability, performance, and fault tolerance to messaging applications. The core of the Service Broker architecture is the *dialog*. A dialog is a reliable, bidirectional, persistent, ordered exchange of messages between two endpoints. An *endpoint* is a SQL Server 2005 database configured for Service Broker messaging. Because the dialog is persistent, it can ensure the messages are processed in the order they were sent, even if the dialog lasts for weeks or months. The dialog messages are stored in database queues to provide asynchronous delivery. Because queues are part of the database, Service Broker messages enjoy all the reliability and fault tolerance that SQL Server supplies for all database data. Service Broker also includes an efficient TCP/IP-based protocol for reliably and securely transferring messages between SQL Server instances.

Benefits of Service Broker Technology

Before diving into the depths of Service Broker technology, let's look at the high-level benefits that Service Broker provides for the SQL Server 2005 application developer:

▶ **Asynchronous actions built into TSQL** — Almost any large, scalable application you work with will perform some functions asynchronously. By the time you're finished with this book, you will be a firm believer that asynchronous execution is absolutely required for an efficient, scaleable system. While SQL Server does much of its internal work asynchronously, before the introduction of Service Broker there was no simple way to write a stored procedure or trigger that would run asynchronously—all calls were synchronous. With Service Broker, the tools you need to build asynchronous applications are included in the TSQL language. This means that writing powerful asynchronous constructs is as easy as writing a select or insert statement.

▶ **Queues as built-in database objects** — When I explain Service Broker to people, I often ask them to think of the biggest database application in their company and then tell me how many tables they have in that application that are used as queues—where rows containing work to be done are inserted into a table by one task and then read by another task and executed. I very seldom run into anyone who says there aren't any queue tables in their application. After discussing their difficulties, performance bottlenecks, and deadlocks, I ask them how much coding effort they would save if they had queues that simply worked, instead of spending weeks trying to make a homegrown queue table work reliably. Most developers who have tried to build their own queue in the database relate to the value of Service Broker. With Service Broker, you can execute a **CREATE QUEUE** statement and have a queue that some of the best minds in SQL Server development have spent years making as fast and reliable as they know how to make it. Chapter 4 explains how Service Broker queues work and how to use them effectively for building asynchronous, queued applications.

▶ **Full database reliability for messages** — In many reliable messaging scenarios, messages contain valuable business data. For example, consider an order entry system that sends reliable messages to a shipping system containing shipment and customer data. If one of those messages is lost, the order won't get shipped and the customer will be upset (especially if the message to the billing system is delivered). Because Service Broker messages are stored in the database, they take advantage of all the data integrity features of SQL Server.

▶ **Reliable message transport** — While many applications require asynchronous operations within a single database or between databases running on the same database server, most large, distributed applications need to execute services on remote servers. Service Broker supports this requirement by providing the reliable transfer of messages between queues on different machines. While reliable messaging is nothing new, reliable messaging between SQL Server databases enables a new class of reliable, distributed database applications.

▶ **New messaging paradigm** — Developers often ask, "If asynchronous applications have so many advantages, why aren't all applications written that way?" The short answer is because asynchronous applications are very hard to get right. Message ordering and multi-reader queue handling are very difficult to get right. Service Broker conversations make writing messaging applications significantly easier. Chapters 2 and 3 explain what conversations are and how to use them effectively to build powerful message-based applications.

▶ **Transactional messaging** — One of the problems in messaging applications is ensuring that messages are processed *exactly once*. We've all seen this problem when we ordered something on the Web. You get everything you want in your shopping cart, give them your address and credit card number, and finally push the button to submit the order. And then you wait with your fingers crossed. If the order acknowledgement screen appears in a few seconds, you know all is well. But what do you do if it doesn't appear? If you push the button again, you might be ordering twice. If you don't, you might not get anything. Service Broker uses reliable, transactional message delivery to ensure that the message will be processed once and only once—even if the network goes down or the data center loses power in the middle of the transaction.

► **Stored procedure activation** — Because receiving a message from a queue is a "pull" operation, the program that is going to receive the message must be running before the message can be received. This often results in programs wasting resources while waiting for messages, or not having enough programs running to handle the volume of messages arriving. The Service Broker answer to this problem is *activation*, which is described in Chapter 8. Activation monitors a Service Broker queue and ensures that when there are messages that require processing, there will be an application running to process them.

► **Deep database integration** — Because Service Broker is part of SQL Server, the database features of SQL Server apply to Service Broker messages. Backing up the database backs up messages. Any high-availability options you use for database data will also apply to messages. You can use ordinary select statements to see what's in a queue. SQL Server traces displayed in Profiler display messaging information along with SQL commands. All this means is that database developers and administrators can use familiar database tools to develop and manage messaging applications.

An Example of Service Broker

I'm a developer at heart, so I always like to start learning about something new by looking at code. Here's a very simple Service Broker application that sends and receives messages. This will give you a feel for how Service Broker applications are put together. The service for this first example is a simple book lookup service that accepts an ISBN number in the request message and returns the name of the book as a response message. This sample always returns the same book name as a response, so it is of limited practical value, but it illustrates how Service Broker services work.

Instead of writing stored procedures or .NET programs, we'll start out by typing commands into a SQL Server Management Studio Window or SQLCMD. This not only makes for a simpler sample, but it emphasizes that Service Broker commands are just extensions to the TSQL language that SQL Server developers use every day. Open up a Management Studio SQL Server Query window and type the code shown in Listing 1.1. For those of you who don't like typing, the code is available online when you register this book at www. rationalpress.com. **Press the F5 key to execute the code.**

```
-- Create a database to work in
CREATE DATABASE PublisherDB
go


USE PublisherDB
go
-- Create the two message types we will use.
CREATE MESSAGE TYPE [ISBNLookupRequest] VALIDATION = NONE
CREATE MESSAGE TYPE [ISBNLookupResponse] VALIDATION = NONE


--   Create a contract for the ISBN Lookup dialog.
CREATE CONTRACT [ISBNLookupContract]
        (
        [ISBNLookupRequest] SENT BY initiator,
        [ISBNLookupResponse] SENT BY target
        )


-- Create the two queues required for this dialog
CREATE QUEUE [ISBNLookupTargetQueue]
CREATE QUEUE [ISBNLookupInitiatorQueue]


-- Create the services for the dialog endpoints.
CREATE SERVICE [ISBNLookupRequestService] ON QUEUE
[ISBNLookupTargetQueue]
        (
        [ISBNLookupContract]
        )
```

```
CREATE SERVICE [ISBNLookupResponseService] ON QUEUE
[ISBNLookupInitiatorQueue]
go
```

Listing 1.1: Creating Service Broker Metadata Objects.

You don't need to spend a lot of time looking at this part of the code to see that we're creating two queues—one for each side of the conversation—and metadata for the conversation. This will all be explained later.

Now let's send a message, as shown in Listing 1.2.

```
USE PublisherDB
go

DECLARE @conversationHandle uniqueidentifier;

BEGIN TRANSACTION;

-- Begin a dialog to the ISBN Lookup Service

BEGIN DIALOG CONVERSATION  @conversationHandle
    FROM SERVICE      [ISBNLookupResponseService]
    TO SERVICE        'ISBNLookupRequestService'
    ON CONTRACT       [ISBNLookupContract]
    WITH LIFETIME = 600;

-- Send a message on the dialog
SEND ON CONVERSATION @conversationHandle
       MESSAGE TYPE [ISBNLookupRequest]
(N'<ISBNLookupRequest>
       <ISBN>0-9726888-1-1</ISBN>
</ISBNLookupRequest>');

COMMIT;
```

Listing 1.2: Sending a Message.

The **BEGIN DIALOG** statement creates a dialog that will be used to send and receive messages. Dialogs are a core concept in Service Broker transactions that are covered in detail in Chapter 2. We then send a message to request information about a book based on its ISBN number. The **SEND** statement puts this message on a queue.

Next, we will receive the message from the queue and send back a response. Open up another query window to represent the receiving application. Run the code in Listing 1.3 to receive the message and send back the response:

```
USE PublisherDB
go


-- Look for messages in the queue
SELECT CAST(message_body AS nvarchar(MAX)) FROM [ISBNLookupTargetQueue]
go


-- Declare the variables we will receive the message data into
DECLARE @conversationHandle uniqueidentifier;
DECLARE @message_body nvarchar(MAX);
DECLARE @message_type_name sysname;


-- Start a transaction
BEGIN TRANSACTION;


-- Receive the message from the queue

RECEIVE TOP(1)
        @message_type_name=message_type_name,
        @conversationHandle=conversation_handle,
        @message_body=message_body
        FROM [ISBNLookupTargetQueue];


PRINT @message_body;


-- If this is a ISBN Lookup message, respond with information about the book.
-- Just return a canned message for now.
IF @message_type_name = N'ISBNLookupRequest'
```

```
        BEGIN

                SEND ON CONVERSATION @conversationHandle
                    MESSAGE TYPE [ISBNLookupResponse]
                    (N'<ISBNLookupResponse>
                        <Title>The Rational Guide to
                        SQL Server Notification Services
                        </Title>
                    </ISBNLookupResponse>');

                -- End the conversation because we're done with it.
                END CONVERSATION @conversationHandle;

        END
-- Commit the transaction
COMMIT
-- The queue should be empty now
SELECT CAST(message_body as nvarchar(MAX)) FROM [ISBNLookupTargetQueue]
go
```

Listing 1.3: Receiving the Message from the Queue and Returning a Response.

First, check the target queue to make sure the message made it to the queue (see Figure 1.1).

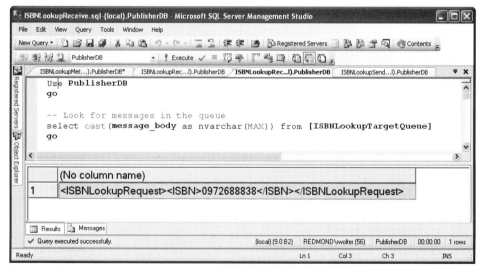

Figure 1.1: Selecting from the Target Queue.

There is a message in the queue, so let's receive it (see Figure 1.2).

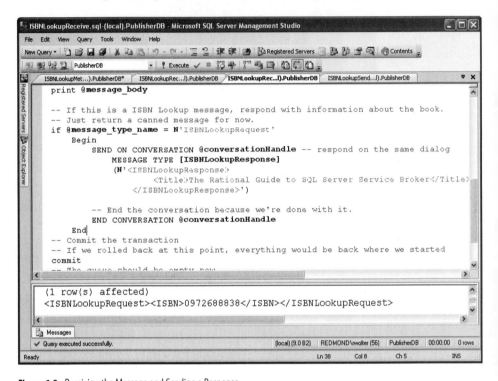

Figure 1.2: Receiving the Message and Sending a Response.

Now go back to the first Management Studio window to receive the response message (see Listing 1.4 and Figure 1.3).

```
USE PublisherDB
go

RECEIVE CAST(message_body as nvarchar(MAX))
    FROM ISBNLookupInitiatorQueue];
```

Listing 1.4: Receiving a Response.

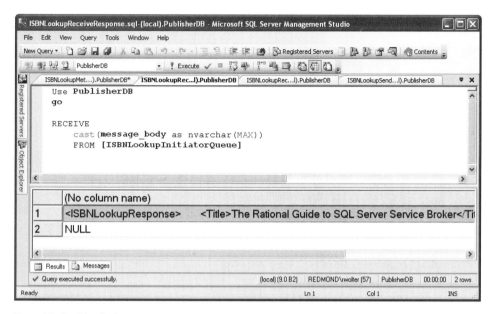

Figure 1.3: Receiving the Response.

Don't try to understand each parameter of every command. We will cover them all in detail later. The purpose of this example is to give you a feel for what Service Broker applications look like.

Summary

This chapter was a quick overview of what Service Broker is and why application developers should learn about this exciting new technology. We also saw our first simple Service Broker application that demonstrated that Service Broker is tightly integrated with SQL Server, so that the whole application was written in TSQL. In the next chapter we will start looking in detail at the database objects that Service Broker uses to implement reliable, asynchronous database operations.

Did you know?

While most people think of Service Broker as an asynchronous messaging system, the combination of asynchronous, ordered messages and the Service Broker activation feature also make it a great task management environment. See Chapter 14 for details.

Chapter 2

Conversations

The core concept in Service Broker is the conversation. Conversations introduce a new messaging paradigm which makes writing reliable distributed applications with Service Broker much easier than with most messaging systems. In most messaging systems, the messaging primitive is the message, but in Service Broker, the messaging primitive is the conversation. In this chapter, you will learn what conversations are and how to use them to make asynchronous applications easier to write.

Conversations and Dialogs

A *conversation* is a reliable, ordered exchange of messages. There are two kinds of conversations defined in the Service Broker architecture:

▶ **Dialog**—A two-way conversation between exactly two endpoints. An *endpoint* is a source or destination for messages associated with a queue and may receive and send messages. A *dialog* is always established between an initiator endpoint and a target endpoint (see Figure 2.1). The *initiator* is the endpoint that issues the **BEGIN DIALOG** command to start the dialog. Other than that, the initiator and target are peers. The first message always goes from the initiator to the target. Once the target receives the first message, any number of messages can be sent in either direction.

▶ **Monolog**—A one-way conversation between a single publisher endpoint and any number of subscriber endpoints. This is a reliable version of the popular publish-subscribe messaging paradigm. However, due to time constraints, monologs are not available in SQL Server 2005, though they will almost certainly be included in future versions.

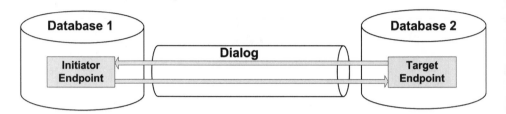

Figure 2.1: Dialog.

Because monologues aren't included in SQL Server 2005, the dialog is the only kind of conversation available and the terms conversation and dialog are essentially synonymous. This could lead to confusion, since you **BEGIN** a dialog and **END** a conversation.

Don't be confused by the inconsistent use of terms. The SQL Server 2005 development team retained the separate terms because when monologs are implemented, we will need to be able to differentiate among conversations, dialogs, and monologs.

This book uses *dialog* when referring to things that are unique to dialogs, and *conversation* when referring to characteristics common to both dialogs and monologs.

Conversations and Message Ordering

The most unique aspect of Service Broker conversations is that they maintain message order throughout the life of the conversation. Most messaging systems only ensure that messages are received in order if they are sent in a single transaction. A Service Broker conversation maintains message order across sending transactions, receiving transactions, and even multiple, parallel, sending and receiving applications.

To see the value of message ordering, think about an application that streams large quantities of video over a network. Getting messages out of order might lead to crimes being solved before they were committed and other strange violations of cause and effect. In a banking application, getting deposits and withdrawals in the wrong order might lead to unjustified overdraft charges. If you write an application where message ordering is important, you will write the logic to ensure that the application can deal with out-of-order messages. The point is that with Service Broker, you don't have to—your application will always receive messages in order.

To preserve order, Service Broker includes a *sequence number* in every message it sends and forces the receiving application to receive messages in the same order they were sent. Some other messaging systems allow messages to be received in any desired order, but Service Broker enforces receive ordering to make the conversation paradigm work correctly.

Reliable Delivery

Service Broker cannot ensure that messages are received in order unless it also ensures they are all received. Missing messages will cause gaps in the sequence, which can't be allowed in a conversation. Service Broker ensures reliable message delivery by resending messages periodically until the message sender receives an acknowledgement. This resending and acknowledgement protocol is built into the Service Broker infrastructure so that the applications sending and receiving the messages aren't aware that it is happening.

As you might imagine, the protocol for sending, resending, and acknowledging messages is quite complex, but it will be sufficient to cover a few of the high points here. See Chapter 9 for more details.

As shown in Figure 2.2, Service Broker messages to be sent over the network are placed temporarily in a queue called the *transmission queue* (**sys.transmission_queue**). Service Broker sends the message over the network and marks it as waiting for an acknowledgement. When Service Broker receives the message at the destination endpoint, it sends an acknowledgement back to the sender. When the sender receives the acknowledgement message, it deletes the message from the transmission queue.

If a message on the transmission queue waits too long for an acknowledgement, it is resent. The definition of "too long" starts at a few seconds and increases every time the message is resent. For those of you who are bothered by the imprecision of this statement, as of the time this chapter was written, the timeout starts at 4 seconds and doubles after every retry until it reaches a maximum of 64 seconds. There are a few performance optimizations built into the protocol to minimize the number of messages exchanged, but this simplified description will suffice for now.

This system of timeouts and retries ensures that messages arrive at their destination in spite of server or network failures. Reliable message delivery means a Service Broker application can send a message and rely on the Service Broker infrastructure to make sure it gets to its destination. The application doesn't have to deal with network failures and retrying failed operations. Once again, Service Broker makes messaging applications easier to write.

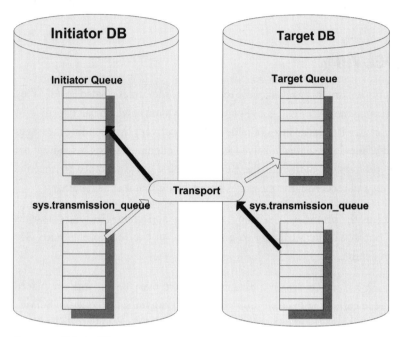

Figure 2.2: Dialogs and Queues.

Symmetric Error Handling

Asynchronous applications are often hard to write because the application requesting a service and the application fulfilling the service request may never execute at the same time. This makes error handling especially hard, because it's possible that one endpoint might disappear because of an error condition without informing the other endpoint.

A Service Broker dialog always has two endpoints with two queues associated with them. This means that the Service Broker logic always knows how to inform both ends of a conversation when an error occurs. We call this aspect of conversation behavior *symmetric error handling*. Symmetric error handling is generally much easier to work with than other messaging systems that make the application monitor dead-letter queues for failed messages.

Conversation Persistence

The reliable, ordered messaging features of Service Broker conversations continue to function through network failures, power failures, and database restarts. To achieve this reliability, Service Broker maintains persistent information about each conversation in both endpoints of the conversation (see Figure 2.3).

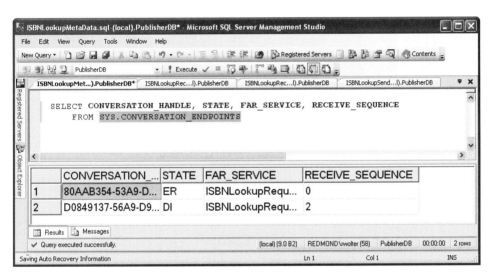

Figure 2.3: Conversation Endpoints.

Look for the persisted information about open conversations in the **sys.conversation_ endpoints** table. If you ran the sample application in Chapter 1, you should still have a conversation open. Try this query:

```
use PublisherDB
select * from sys.conversation_endpoints
```

Most of the columns won't make sense yet. I'll explain a few columns now and cover the rest later.

> ▶ **conversation_handle**—This is a uniqueidentifer that refers to the conversation in TSQL commands. This is the primary key for the row.

► **conversation_id**—This is the "on the wire" identifier for a conversation. This identifier is included in each message sent across the network. Each message of this conversation has this uniqueidentifier in its header so that the endpoint knows which conversation the message belongs to. At this point, you are probably wondering when to use the conversation_handle instead of another uniqueidentifier. When both endpoints of a conversation are in the same database (as they were in the ISBN Lookup example in Chapter 1), there will be two rows in the table for the same conversation. Therefore, we need two handles as keys. The **is_initiator** flag indicates which endpoint is the initiator for the dialog.

► **receive_sequence**—This is the next sequence number that should be received at this endpoint.

► **send_sequence**—This is the next sequence number to be sent from this endpoint.

► **receive_sequence_frag**— Service Broker messages can be up to 2 GB in size, but sending a message that big could tie up the network connection for a minute or more. To avoid monopolizing the network with a very large message, large messages are split into 90 KB fragments and then assembled on the receiving end. The **receive_sequence_frag** field in the conversation endpoint keeps track of how many fragments of the next message have been received.

Because the message sequence numbers are tracked in a database table, message order in a conversation can be maintained through database restarts, recovery from backup, and failover—even if the conversation lasts for months or years.

Beginning and Ending Conversations

Before sending a Service Broker message, you must create a dialog conversation. An example of the command to create a simple dialog is shown in Listing 2.1:

```
BEGIN DIALOG CONVERSATION  @conversationHandle
    FROM SERVICE      [ISBNLookupResponseService]
    TO SERVICE        'ISBNLookupRequestService'
    ON CONTRACT       [ISBNLookupContract]
    WITH LIFETIME = 600;
```

Listing 2.1: Creating a Dialog.

The **@conversation_handle** variable is used to return a uniqueidentifier, which will be used to refer to the dialog in any future Service Broker statements that use this dialog.

Because dialogs always connect exactly two endpoints, you must specify both endpoints in the **BEGIN DIALOG** command. Endpoints are specified using service names. A *service* is a name for an endpoint. Services will be covered in more detail in Chapter 5.

The *contract* defines the message content of a dialog. Only messages specified in the definition of a contract may be sent on a dialog. Contracts are discussed in Chapter 5.

The **LIFETIME** clause specifies the number of seconds that this dialog is allowed to live. If a dialog still exists after the lifetime expires (10 minutes in this case), an error will be returned to any statements that attempt to access it and error messages are sent to both endpoints of the dialog. It is important to realize that the dialog doesn't go away when its lifetime expires. It remains in the **sys.conversation_endpoints** table in an error state until it is ended.

Dialog conversations are persistent database objects which exist until both ends of the conversation are ended. Conversations are ended with the following command:

```
END CONVERSATION @conversationHandle
```

Because both endpoints of the conversation must be ended, this command must be issued from both endpoints before the conversation ends completely.

If you look at the example in Chapter 1, you will notice that only one end of the conversation was ended. In Figure 2.3, you can see one conversation with a state of "DI" (meaning "disconnected inbound"), indicating that the opposite endpoint was ended with an **END CONVERSATION** command but this endpoint of the conversation hasn't been ended yet.

The other conversation state is "ER" (or "error") because it has been open long enough that the timeout has expired and the conversation ended with an error. If you execute an **END CONVERSATION** command specifying the conversation_handle for the row in the **sys.conversation_endpoints** table, it will go away.

Remembering to end all conversations is a very important programming practice. If you forget to do this, you will find thousands of rows in the **sys.conversation_endpoints** table after your application has run for awhile. Conversations are cached for performance, so too many of them will use excessive memory and tempdb space.

On the other hand, it is important not to end the conversation until you are done with it. The rich ordering features of conversations are not very useful if you start a new dialog for every message. After all, any messaging system can process a single message in order. To use Service Broker to its full potential, be sure to keep conversations open for as long as necessary.

Note:

Secure dialogs (any dialog started without the ENCRYPTION = OFF option) require that the database where they are started have a database master key. You can create a master key with the following command (use your own password, of course):

```
CREATE MASTER KEY ENCRYPTION BY PASSWORD ='aspof>8#8!:|'
```

Summary

Conversations are one of the fundamental concepts of Service Broker. There are two types of conversations (monologs and dialogs), but only dialogs are included in SQL Server 2005. A dialog is a reliable, two-way, ordered, persistent exchange of messages between two endpoints. The fundamental communications primitive for most messaging systems is a message. For Service Broker, the messaging primitive is the dialog.

Chapter 3

Conversation Groups

In the last chapter, we learned that Service Broker conversations ensure that messages on the same conversation are processed in order. In this chapter we will learn how that is done.

Conversations ensure that messages are processed in order. While it is reasonably straightforward to ensure that messages are received in order, it is more difficult to ensure that they are processed in order. To see why this is a problem, think of a large, multi-threaded application receiving and processing order entry messages. One thread will receive the order header message and start processing it. In the meantime, other threads may receive order line messages associated with this order. Because order lines are quicker to process (one insert for an order line as opposed to multiple inserts and updates for an order header), the order line message transaction will often commit first and then fail, because there is no corresponding order header.

Even though messages are received in order, a multi-threaded application may not process them in order. Writing an application that works correctly with messages that are processed out of order and processed on multiple threads simultaneously can be very difficult. For this reason, many message processing applications are single-threaded. While this solves the ordering problem, it has a severe impact on the scalability of the application.

Service Broker gets around this issue by using a special kind of lock to ensure that only one task can read messages from a particular conversation at a time. This ensures that a multi-threaded application that receives messages in order will also process them in order. This special lock is called a *conversation group lock*.

Conversation Group Locking

It's easy to see the value of locking a conversation during message processing, but there are some cases where this isn't enough. For example, imagine an order entry application that sends messages to credit card validation, inventory adjustment, shipping, and accounts receivable services on four different dialogs. These services may all respond at roughly the same time, so it's possible that response messages for the same order may be processed on different threads simultaneously. This can cause problems. If two different transactions update the order status simultaneously without being aware of each other, status information may be lost.

To solve this problem, Service Broker locks conversation groups—not conversations. By default, a *conversation group* contains a single conversation, so conversation group locking equates to conversation locking. If your application can benefit from locking more than one conversation at a time, you may expand the conversation group by adding more conversations to it.

There are several ways to group dialogs into the same conversation group. Any time you **BEGIN** a dialog, Service Broker will automatically (by default) create a conversation group for it. To see this, run the query shown in Listing 3.1.

```
Declare @ISBNHandle UniqueIdentifier
BEGIN DIALOG  @ISBNHandle
    FROM SERVICE     [ISBNLookupResponseService]
    TO SERVICE       'ISBNLookupRequestService'
    ON CONTRACT      [ISBNLookupContract]
    WITH LIFETIME = 600;
select conversation_group_id from sys.conversation_endpoints where
    conversation_handle = @ISBNHandle
select * from sys.conversation_groups
```

Listing 3.1: Creating a Conversation Group.

You should see a row in the **sys.conversation_groups** table that matches the row in the **sys.conversation_endpoints** table for the conversation you just created. This row is the row that Service Broker locks when it receives messages from any of the conversations in the conversation group.

Notice that Service Broker locks the row in the **sys.conversation_groups** table—not the **sys.conversation_endpoints** table or the queue. This means that if more messages are received for the conversation, they can be added to the conversation while the conversation group is locked. The **sys.conversation_endpoints** row isn't locked, so it can be changed while the conversation group is locked.

Figure 3.1 below shows how a lock on a conversation group effectively locks a whole group of related messages. Because all Service Broker commands check the conversation group lock before accessing any messages in the queue, the transaction that holds the conversation group lock has exclusive access to all the conversations and messages associated with the conversation group. At the same time, the Service Broker background processes are free to add new messages to the queue and update the conversation state because they are not blocked by the conversation group lock.

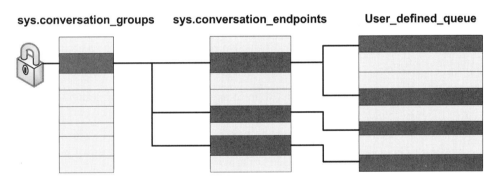

Figure 3.1: Conversation Group Locking.

To initiate multiple conversations in the same conversation group, you first begin one dialog that will automatically create a conversation group. You then expand the conversation group by beginning additional dialogs related to the first one, as shown in Listing 3.2.

```
Declare @ISBNHandle UniqueIdentifier, @Pricehandle UniqueIdentifier
BEGIN DIALOG  @ISBNHandle
    FROM SERVICE    [ISBNLookupResponseService]
    TO SERVICE      'ISBNLookupRequestService'
    ON CONTRACT     [ISBNLookupContract]
    WITH LIFETIME = 600;
BEGIN DIALOG  @PriceHandle
    FROM SERVICE    [PriceLookupResponseService]
    TO SERVICE      'PriceLookupRequestService'
    ON CONTRACT     [PriceLookupContract]
    WITH RELATED_CONVERSATION = @ISBNHandle, LIFETIME = 600;
```

Listing 3.2: Initiating Multiple Conversations in the Same Conversation Group.

The same technique works when you wish to associate new dialogs with a conversation_ handle you obtained from a **RECEIVE** statement. For example, in our order entry scenario, the credit verification dialog is related to the conversation_handle obtained when the order header is received.

Finally, there may be cases where you want to assign the conversation group identifier yourself. For example, you may want the conversation group ID to be a unique identifier you already use in your program. You do this by associating the new dialog you are creating with a conversation group ID of your choosing, as shown in Listing 3.3.

```
Declare @ISBNHandle UniqueIdentifier, @ISBNGroup UniqueIdentifier

SET @ISBNGroup = NewID()

BEGIN DIALOG  @ISBNHandle
    FROM SERVICE    [ISBNLookupResponseService]
    TO SERVICE      'ISBNLookupRequestService'
    ON CONTRACT     [ISBNLookupContract]
    WITH RELATED_CONVERSATION_GROUP = @ISBNGroup, LIFETIME = 600;
```

Listing 3.3: Associating a New Dialog with a Conversation Group of Your Choosing.

Choosing Effective Groupings

As we have seen, conversation group locking prevents data integrity problems caused by processing related messages simultaneously on different threads. To take advantage of this feature, you must design your application so that any messages that shouldn't be processed simultaneously are in the same conversation group. In general, you should make sure that a conversation group contains the dialogs for any messages that cause updates to the same data.

On the other hand, if dialogs contain messages that don't update any common data, they don't need the protection of conversation group locking. Placing these dialogs in different conversation groups will allow parallel processing and may improve performance.

Tech Tip:

While conversation group locking is one of the most powerful features of Service Broker, many simple applications don't need to use it. If you can't come up with a reason why two dialogs should not be processed in parallel, don't put them in the same conversation group.

When first learning about conversation group locking, new users sometimes get the impression that Service Broker applications are single-threaded and thus won't scale. In a Service Broker order entry application, all the dialogs used to process an order are in the same conversation group. This means that the order entry application will process all the messages for an individual order serially, but any number of different orders can be processed in parallel. This generally improves performance because the application doesn't have to deal with issues caused by related messages processed on different threads. Because Service Broker handles the locking for you, it gives you the simplicity of a single-threaded programming model while still letting your application scale to as many threads as you need.

Another common misconception is that conversation groups apply to the remote endpoints of conversations. For example, someone will initiate two conversations in the same group and then expect them to be in the same group at the target endpoint. Conversation groups exist only in the queue where they were created. The two endpoints of a conversation will always be part of different conversation groups.

Summary

Service Broker ensures that messages in the same conversation can't be processed in parallel by locking the conversation during the transaction that processes the messages. Many applications can benefit from extending this lock to cover a group of related conversations—for example, all the conversations related to a particular order in an order entry application. Service Broker supports conversation groups to represent related conversations and conversation group locking to lock related conversations.

Chapter 4

Queues

So far we have talked about *why* Service Broker performs asynchronously. This chapter covers *how* Service Broker performs asynchronous operations. In asynchronous processing, you request some processing now and the system does it later. Between the time you request the operation and the time the system does it, the request must be stored somewhere. We call that storage place a *queue*.

Service Broker implements queues with a new feature of SQL Server 2005 called *hidden tables*. Queues look just like normal tables to the storage engine, but the normal TSQL commands can't be used to manipulate the data in them. You can't use **INSERT**, **DELETE**, or **UPDATE** commands on queues and you can't change the queue structure or create triggers on queues. There is a read-only view associated with every queue, so you can use a **SELECT** statement to see what messages are in the queue. This is much easier than many messaging systems, which require you to "peek" the messages one at a time to see what is in the queue.

Queues make reliable asynchronous messaging possible. The message sender puts a message on a queue and goes on to handle other requests. The transport logic then moves the message reliably to the destination queue. The receiving application can then pull the message off the queue at its leisure. The message isn't deleted from the first queue until it has been stored successfully in a destination (second) queue, so there's no chance it will be lost in transit. Refer to Figure 2.2 in Chapter 2 to refresh your memory about the relationship between queues and dialogs.

Because Service Broker queues are implemented as hidden database tables, Service Broker messages share all the high-availability features that safeguard SQL Server data. All the features that you use to ensure that your SQL Server data isn't lost or damaged— transactions, logging, backup, mirroring, clustering, and so on—also apply to Service Broker messages.

In many reliable messaging applications, messages are valuable business objects. In our publishing scenario, for example, the shipment and billing messages are sent to the shipping and billing service. If these messages are lost, books will not be shipped or shipments will not be billed—both potentially damaging to the business. Queues in the database ensure that these valuable messages won't be lost unless the database itself is lost or damaged.

Creating, Enabling and Disabling Queues

Since a queue is a database object like a table, the command to create a queue resembles the command to create a table:

```
CREATE QUEUE [ISBNLookupTargetQueue]
```

The main difference is that you don't have to define the columns of a queue, because all queues have the same columns. Books Online has a complete listing of the columns, or you can use a **SELECT** * FROM <queue-name> to see what columns it uses.

Like a table, you can specify a filegroup to store the queue data. You might want to put queues on their own disk drive if you expect them to grow very big or if you expect a lot of activity on the queue. You can also specify whether a queue should be active by using the **STATUS = ON|OFF** clause. If the queue status is **OFF**, Service Broker will not place messages on the queue and applications will not read messages from the queue. Messages that arrive for the queue will be held on the transmission queue until the queue status is changed to **ON**.

The **RETENTION** option determines whether messages are deleted from the queue when the transaction that receives the messages commits. If **RETENTION** is **ON**, Service Broker retains all messages sent to the queue and all messages sent by services associated with the queue until the conversation that owns them ends. Some applications that deal with long-running conversations turn **RETENTION** on, so that if an error is encountered, they will know what has happened in the conversation and what actions need to be undone. For example, if a conversation decreases the inventory of a particular book by 20 and then finds that the order can't be shipped because the customer's credit is bad, the error handling routine will have to put the 20 books back into available inventory. If the message that reduced the inventory quantity has been retained in the queue, the error routine can easily find which changes have to be undone. The **RETENTION = ON** option can cause queues to grow very large and may significantly reduce performance, so you should set **RETENTION = ON** only when necessary. For many applications, keeping a state table that tracks pending conversations may be more efficient than the retention option.

Use the following command to create a disabled queue with the **RETENTION** option turned on:

```
CREATE QUEUE [OrderBookQueue]
   WITH
      STATUS = OFF,
      RETENTION = ON
   ON QueueFilegroup
```

The following command would turn **RETENTION OFF**:

```
ALTER QUEUE [OrderBookQueue]
   WITH RETENTION = OFF
```

Examining Queues in a Database

In this section you will learn how to find queues in the database and query the queues to find out what messages are on each queue. To see the queues we created in Chapter 1, run this query:

```
use publisherdb;
select name, object_id, is_ms_shipped, is_receive_enabled,
is_enqueue_enabled, is_retention_enabled from sys.service_queues
```

If you have been following along with the examples in the book, you will see the queues you created when you ran previous samples and three queues that you didn't create (see Figure 4.1). These three extra queues should have a 1 in the **is_ms_shipped** column, meaning they were created when the database was created. They are used by the Query Notification and Event Notification features in SQL Server 2005.

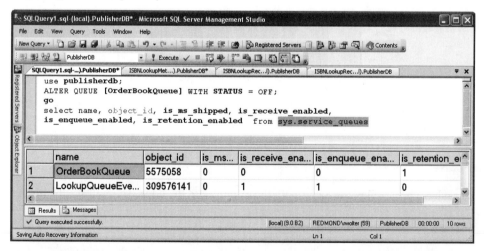

Figure 4.1: Service Queues.

A 1 in the **is_receive_enabled** and **is_enqueue_enabled** columns means that the queue is enabled. To prove this, run the following query and then look at the queues again.

```
ALTER QUEUE [OrderBookQueue] WITH STATUS = OFF;
```

Both flags are changed when the queue is enabled or disabled (see Figure 4.2). Future versions of Service Broker should allow you to enable **is_receive_enabled** and **is_enqueue_enabled** separately.

Figure 4.2: Disabled Queue.

To see what the queue itself looks like, run this query:

```
use publisherdb
select * from ISBNLookupInitiatorQueue
```

Chances are, the only messages in this queue are error messages informing you that the conversation lifetime has expired. You will notice that the message body isn't very readable, because the message body is a **varbinary(MAX)** field. What you see is the binary representation of the XML text. To see what the messages say, try casting the message_body to XML:

```
select cast(message_body as XML) Body from ISBNLookupInitiatorQueue
```

If you are using Management Studio to run the queries, clicking on the XML should display it in a nicely formatted view, as shown in Figure 4.3.

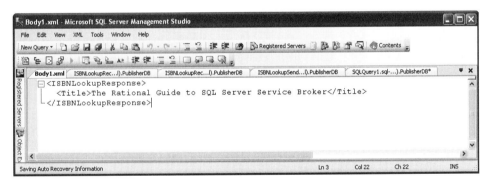

Figure 4.3: XML-Formatted Message.

When Service Broker needs to temporarily store a message on the way to the destination queue, it puts it on a *transmission queue*. Each database has a transmission queue named **sys.transmission_queue**. The script shown in Listing 4.1 will put a message on the transmission queue:

```
Use PublisherDB
DECLARE @conversationHandle uniqueidentifier
Begin Transaction
BEGIN DIALOG  @conversationHandle
    FROM SERVICE    [ISBNLookupResponseService]
    TO SERVICE      'BogusService'
    ON CONTRACT     [ISBNLookupContract]
    WITH ENCRYPTION = OFF, LIFETIME = 600;
SEND ON CONVERSATION @conversationHandle
        MESSAGE TYPE [ISBNLookupRequest]
(N'SendMessage')
commit
select * from sys.transmission_queue
```

Listing 4.1: Placing a Message on a Transmission Queue.

Notice that the **TO SERVICE** value ('BogusService') doesn't exist. This ensures that the message will stay in the transmission queue. In cases where a message cannot be delivered, Service Broker tries to hold messages and retry rather than error the conversation. Because messages are valuable business data, Service Broker does not error a conversation for things that might be transient network problems or configuration problems that can be corrected by an administrator.

As you can see, most of the columns in the transmission queue are the same as in user-defined queues. The most interesting difference is the **transmission_status** column, which contains the current error for each message in the transmission queue. You should always check this column if messages are not delivered promptly.

Summary

Service Broker makes reliable, asynchronous database applications possible by providing queues that are tightly integrated into the SQL Server database. This tight integration includes the conversation group locking covered in Chapter 3 and queue manipulation operations added to the TSQL language. Database queues that "just work" are a powerful new tool for database application development.

Chapter 5

Service Broker Metadata

Service Broker uses several new SQL Server metadata types to simplify the task of writing an asynchronous application. These objects are all pure metadata objects, which means they don't have any storage assigned to them the way tables and indexes do. They are similar to constraints in that they define valid data values for other commands. This chapter begins with a discussion of naming conventions for Service Broker objects that make it easier to ensure unique names for a distributed Service Broker application. The following sections describe each metadata object, explaining how it fits into the Service Broker programming model, and how to create the object.

Naming

Service Broker metadata names are always case-sensitive. These names use binary collation (byte-by-byte matching) because the names are sent over the network in messages from one SQL Server instance to another. The sending and receiving database will often have different default collations, so binary collation is used to ensure that the name of the metadata object will match the name in the message no matter what collations the sending and receiving databases use.

Most Service Broker samples and examples use URLs as metadata names to ensure that names will be unique when conversations span distributed systems. [http://RoadRunner. com/PurchaseOrder] and [http://Coyote.com/PurchaseOrder] are obviously different URLs, but if they both had the name **PurchaseOrder**, it would be impossible to know if they were different.

URLs aren't required, but unless you are sure your application will never be distributed, it is a good practice to use them. You may use any technique you want to ensure uniqueness.

The SQL Server development team recommends URLs because they're easy to remember and usually unique. For the built-in metadata objects, they used the same URL as the XML Namespaces in SQL Server. Although these all start with http://, it's generally best to avoid the http: prefix because it makes users think there should be a Web page at the URL address. Also, remember that URLs contain characters that aren't valid in SQL Server names, so you must enclose them in brackets [].

Message Types

A message type labels the contents of a Service Broker message. The SQL data type for all Service Broker messages is **varbinary(MAX)**—a bucket of up to two GB of whatever data the application wants to put into it. Service Broker applications use the message type associated with the message to determine what the message contains.

Here's a command to create a simple message type with only a name:

```
CREATE MESSAGE TYPE ISBNLookup
```

The name of a message type is just a SQL Server identifier. Any valid name will suffice, but the convention is to use a URL for the name. Many applications only need a label for each message type.

In some applications you may want to restrict the valid values that a message body may have. This is done by adding a **VALIDATION** clause to the **CREATE** command. For example, if the message body is an XML document, you can associate an XML Schema collection with the message type and the Service Broker logic will validate all messages received at an endpoint with the schemas in the collection. The command for specifying XML schema validation looks like this:

```
CREATE MESSAGE TYPE ISBNLookup
  VALIDATION = VALID_XML WITH SCHEMA COLLECTION ISBNSchemas;
```

A Schema Collection is a new object in SQL Server 2005 that contains one or more XML Schemas. Because the collection can contain several schemas, you can put all the schemas required for an application into the same collection so they can be easily distributed and maintained. Refer to the **CREATE SCHEMA COLLECTION** command in Books Online for more information on schema collections.

The validation clause can also specify **WELL_FORMED_XML** or **EMPTY**. When **WELL_FORMED_XML** is specified, the receiving endpoint will load the XML into an XML parser to ensure that it can be parsed. Specifying a value of **EMPTY** validates that the message body is NULL. If a message fails validation, it is discarded and an error message is sent back to the sender. Note that the message is only validated on the receiving side of the conversation. Messages can be sent successfully that will fail validation when they reach the destination.

The two XML validations load every message of that type into an XML parser when each is received. This obviously affects performance. If you are receiving messages from untrusted sources and the message volume isn't high, validation may make sense. However, if the application loads the message body into a parser before processing the message, it may be more efficient to handle parsing or validation errors in the application rather than parsing the message body twice.

The **ALTER MESSAGE TYPE** command can turn validation off, so it makes sense to turn validation on during development and then turn it off before deployment.

Contracts

A Service Broker *contract* restricts which Message Types appear in a conversation. A contract simplifies application development because an application developer can look at the contract definition to determine which message types can be received and sent on the conversation. Applications don't have to implement logic to handle unexpected message types arriving on the conversation, because Service Broker will only deliver message types specified in the contract.

The contract also determines whether a Message Type may be sent by the initiator of the conversation, sent by the target of the conversation, or sent by either the initiator or target. The following command creates a simple contract for a request-response application where the initiator sends one type of message to the target and the target responds with another Message Type:

```
CREATE CONTRACT ISBNcontract
   ( ISBNLookup SENT BY INITIATOR, ISBNLookupResp SENT BY TARGET ) ;
```

Because adding or deleting a message type could break applications written to use a contract, the **ALTER CONTRACT** command can not change the Message Type information of a contract.

The first message sent from the initiator to the target of the dialog creates the dialog on the target side, so one of the Message Types included in a contract must be sent by the initiator.

Services

A Service Broker service identifies an endpoint of a conversation. An endpoint is a queue in a database. The **BEGIN DIALOG** command specifies a "**FROM SERVICE**" service name and a "**TO SERVICE**" service name. These service names define which queues receive messages at each endpoint of the conversation.

Why not just use the queue name instead of using a service name as an alias for a queue? A Service Broker service might represent multiple queues load-balanced to multiple machines, or a queue may move to a different machine. Because the application only needs to know the names of the services it uses, changes to the infrastructure that implements the service don't require changes to the application.

The service metadata object also includes a list of the contracts that are accepted by the service. An attempt to begin a dialog to a service using a contract not listed in the **CREATE SERVICE** command will fail.

The following command will create a service on the **OrderBookQueue** queue that will accept dialogs opened with the **ISBNcontract** contract.

```
CREATE SERVICE ISBNService ON QUEUE [OrderBookQueue]
    ( ISBNcontract );
```

The Service Broker metadata has referential integrity constraints to prevent the dropping of objects in use by other objects. Message Types in use by contracts can not be dropped, and contracts in use by services can not be dropped. Objects must be dropped in reverse order of creation.

Figure 5.1 shows the relationships among the metadata objects used by Service Broker.

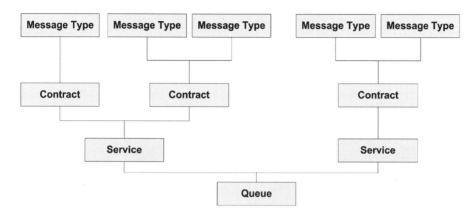

Figure 5.1: Service Broker Metadata Objects.

These queries will display the Service Broker metadata objects in a database:

```
select * from sys.service_message_types
select * from sys.service_contracts
select * from sys.services
select * from sys.service_contract_message_usages
select * from sys.service_contract_usages
```

Each query accesses the catalog view that exposes the metadata object stored in the database's system tables. The columns correspond to the attributes of each metadata object. Use these queries to ensure the metadata objects you create have the attributes they need, or use them to find out about the metadata of an existing Service Broker application.

Default Messages and Contracts

Service Broker includes some built-in metadata that you can use to simplify applications when it's not critical to the application to know the message type of received messages. One example of this type of application is one where all messages are processed by the same logic, either because the messages are all the same or because the application differentiates between messages types by examining the message contents.

The name of the default Message Type is **DEFAULT**. The **DEFAULT** Message Type is associated with the **DEFAULT** contract. If you wish to use the **DEFAULT** contract you must include it in the definition of the **TARGET** service:

```
CREATE SERVICE [ISBNRequestService] ON QUEUE [ISBNTargetQueue]
  ( [DEFAULT] )
```

Notice that **DEFAULT** is a SQL Server keyword so it must be escaped as **[DEFAULT]** when used as a contract name.

The **DEFAULT** contract and message type are always in scope, so they do not have to be specified in the **BEGIN DIALOG** and **SEND** statements:

```
BEGIN DIALOG  @conversationHandle
    FROM SERVICE    [ISBNResponseService]
    TO SERVICE      'ISBNRequestService';
```

and

```
SEND ON CONVERSATION @conversationHandle
(N'This is a test.  This is only a test')
```

Summary

Service Broker uses information stored in SQL Server metadata objects to define the contents of messages and how messages are combined in conversations. This means that an application developer can look at the metadata for a Service Broker service to determine what messages to expect when receiving data from a Service Broker queue.

Developing Service Broker Applications

Chapter 6

Service Broker Programming Basics

This chapter demonstrates how to write basic Service Broker programs using the concepts covered in the preceding chapters. For simplicity's sake, all the examples will be in TSQL. While the Service Broker commands are all TSQL commands, most significant Service Broker applications are written in a higher level language like C#, VB, or C++ because TSQL isn't suitable for complex processing.

Many of the sample applications that are shipped with SQL Server 2005 are written in higher level languages. The sample applications include a CLR library that wraps the Service Broker functions in a user-friendly object model. If your applications are going to be written in one of the CLR languages, I would recommend learning and using the sample library. This interface wasn't incorporated into the .NET libraries because the WCF (Windows Communication Foundation) interfaces are the future direction for Visual Studio. This book doesn't use the library because it hides many of the details that are important for you to see while you are learning. However, once you understand the basics, the sample library will eliminate much of the routine code that all messaging applications share.

This chapter starts with a detailed examination of the **SEND** and **RECEIVE** commands that form the core of any Service Broker application. It then explains how to use these commands to build Service Broker applications. Chapters 7 and 8 cover common extensions to the basic application model presented in this chapter.

Sending and Receiving Messages

Thus far, this book has not talked about distributed Service Broker applications, so the messages we send and receive in this chapter won't leave the database. This is an important concept to understand. In asynchronous messaging, **SEND** means to put a message on a queue and **RECEIVE** means to pull a message off a queue. Between the **SEND** and the **RECEIVE**, the system may or may not move the message from one queue to another queue, but the power of the asynchronous messaging programming model is that the application looks the same whether the queues are in the same database or thousands of miles apart, or whether the **RECEIVE** happens milliseconds or weeks after the **SEND.**

Figure 6.1 shows the basic flow of commands and messages in a simple Service Broker dialog.

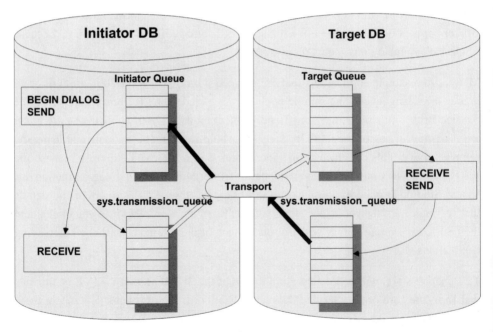

Figure 6.1: Commands and Messages in a Service Broker Dialog.

The SEND Command

Sending a message always happens in the context of a conversation. Therefore, before you send a message, you must obtain a conversation handle. If you are the initiator of a conversation, you obtain a conversation handle by executing a **BEGIN DIALOG** command. The target of a conversation obtains a conversation handle from a **RECEIVE** statement. Here's a basic **SEND** statement:

```
SEND ON CONVERSATION @ConversationHandle
   MESSAGE TYPE [ISBNLookupRequest]
   (@Message);
```

SEND has only three parameters:

▶ A conversation handle associated with an open conversation.

▶ A message type that describes the contents of the message.

▶ The message body itself, which is a SQL Server scalar expression that must evaluate to a SQL Server datatype that can be cast as **varbinary(MAX)**. The **SEND** command explicitly casts the message body parameter to **varbinary(MAX)**.

Remember that a **SEND** command puts a message on a queue. In fact, a **SEND** command translates to an **INSERT** command into the hidden table behind the queue. You supply three of the queue columns as parameters to the **SEND** command and Service Broker fills in the rest of the queue columns based on the dialog parameters and metadata.

The RECEIVE Command

The **RECEIVE** command pulls one or more messages from a queue. The syntax of the basic **RECEIVE** command is very similar to a **SELECT** command:

```
RECEIVE conversation_handle, message_type_name, message_body
   FROM [ISBNLookupInitiatorQueue]
```

A **RECEIVE** command can return up to 15 columns, but the three shown here are all that's needed for the samples in this chapter. To get the complete list, try the following code:

```
RECEIVE * FROM [ISBNLookupInitiatorQueue]
```

Even though the syntax looks a lot like a **SELECT** statement, the **RECEIVE** command is significantly different in that a given message can only be received once. Once a successful **RECEIVE** is committed, the message can't be received again. In reality, **RECEIVE** translates to a **DELETE** command with the **OUTPUT** option.

A **RECEIVE** command doesn't retrieve all the messages on the queue. It locks the first available conversation group that has messages available and is not locked by another **RECEIVE** command and returns the messages from the locked conversation group.

The WAITFOR Command

The basic **RECEIVE** command returns the messages available at the time the command executes. If the queue is empty, no rows are returned. In some cases it might be more efficient to wait for messages to appear on the queue rather than returning immediately when the queue is empty. Use the **WAITFOR** clause with the **RECEIVE** command to force the **RECEIVE** command to wait for a message if the queue is empty. Adding the **WAITFOR** clause to the **RECEIVE** command looks like this:

```
WAITFOR (
    RECEIVE conversation_handle, message_type_name, message_body
        FROM [ISBNLookupInitiatorQueue]
) , TIMEOUT 2000;
```

The **TIMEOUT** clause specifies how many milliseconds the **RECEIVE** will wait for a message to appear on the queue before returning. A **WAITFOR** with no timeout means the **RECEIVE** will wait for a message no matter how long it takes. Waiting for a message to appear on the queue is generally more efficient than polling the queue by using the **RECEIVE** command periodically. The main exception to this would be a low priority queue that is only polled for messages periodically when higher priority queues are empty.

The TOP Clause

The **RECEIVE** command also accepts a **TOP** clause to control the number of messages returned. Retrieving all the messages available utilizes fewer server resources than multiple **RECEIVE** commands, so you should avoid the **TOP** clause whenever possible. The main reason to use the **TOP** clause is in stored procedures where receiving one message at a time into TSQL variables simplifies programming, or when there's a chance that a **RECEIVE** command will retrieve more messages than you want to process in a single transaction. Here's an example of a **RECEIVE** command with a **TOP** clause.

```
RECEIVE TOP (1)
    @ConversationHandle = conversation_handle,
    @MessageType = message_type_name,
    @Message = message_body
    FROM [ISBNLookupInitiatorQueue]
```

The **RECEIVE** command also supports receiving into a table variable. This helps make up for not supporting cursors on a **RECEIVE** command. The following command **RECEIVE's** all the messages available on the queue from the next available conversation group into a table variable called **receive_table.**

```
DECLARE @receive_table TABLE(handle UNIQUEIDENTIFIER,
    message_type_name NVARCHAR(256), message_body VARBINARY(MAX));
RECEIVE conversation_handle, message_type_name, message_body
    FROM [ISBNLookupInitiatorQueue] INTO @receive_table;
```

The WHERE Clause

The **RECEIVE** statement also includes a **WHERE** clause, but it isn't the full-featured **WHERE** clause that you're used to. With **RECEIVE**, the only thing you can specify is a conversation_handle or conversation_group_id.

Specifying a conversation_group_id is useful if you are processing messages from a particular conversation group and you want to see if there are any more related messages on the queue. The following **RECEIVE** statement will only find messages in the conversation group identified by *@ConversationGroupID*:

```
RECEIVE TOP (1)
   @ConversationHandle = conversation_handle,
   @MessageType = message_type_name,
   @Message = message_body
   FROM [ISBNLookupInitiatorQueue]
   WHERE conversation_group_id = @ConversationGroupID
```

Use a **WHERE** clause with the conversation_handle if you know which conversation you want to receive a message on. User interface applications often send a message to be processed and then wait for a response message. A **RECEIVE** statement specifying the same conversation_handle as the one specified in the **SEND** statement will wait until that specific conversation returns a message. Be sure that the **SEND** transaction commits before you call **RECEIVE**. The example in Listing 6.1 **sends** a message to a remote service, commits the **SEND** transaction, and waits for the response message to return.

```
DECLARE @ConversationHandle uniqueidentifier
SELECT TOP (1) @ConversationHandle = conversation_handle
FROM sys.conversation_endpoints
DECLARE @MessageType sysname
DECLARE @Message XML
BEGIN TRANSACTION
SET @Message = Cast((select * from sys.services for xml auto) as XML)
BEGIN DIALOG  @conversationHandle
    FROM SERVICE    [ISBNLookupResponseService]
    TO SERVICE      'ISBNLookupRequestService'
    ON CONTRACT     [ISBNLookupContract];

SEND ON CONVERSATION @ConversationHandle
   MESSAGE TYPE [ISBNLookupRequest]
   (@Message);
COMMIT

BEGIN TRANSACTION
WAITFOR (
RECEIVE TOP (1)
```

```
   @MessageType = message_type_name,
   @Message = message_body
   FROM [ISBNLookupInitiatorQueue]
   WHERE conversation_handle = @ConversationHandle
);
COMMIT
```

Listing 6.1: Waiting for the Response Message.

Using an asynchronous connection to do a synchronous operation is a pretty inefficient use of resources but this is sometimes necessary in client applications. The **RECEIVE** statement will tie up SQL Server resources while it is waiting for a response, so avoid waiting for a specific conversation unless you don't have another choice.

Another common use of the conversation_handle in the **WHERE** clause is to receive a message that you have identified by using a **SELECT** from the queue view. This is also a pretty inefficient use of resources, so you shouldn't do this as a general practice, but some applications need to do this to control which messages are processed first. Remember that messages on a dialog have to be processed in order, so if the message you want isn't the next available message in the dialog, you will have to receive and process the messages ahead of it on the dialog. If you find yourself doing this regularly, you're using one dialog where you should be using more than one.

Keywords

One of the stranger aspects of the **SEND** and **RECEIVE** commands is that while they were added as TSQL commands, they were not made terminal keywords. This was done to avoid breaking current applications that use **SEND** or **RECEIVE** as names. For example, this still works in SQL Server 2005, as shown in Listing 6.2.

```
CREATE TABLE SEND (char_column char)
INSERT INTO SEND VALUES('a')
SELECT * FROM SEND

CREATE PROCEDURE RECEIVE AS
SELECT * FROM sys.databases
go
EXEC RECEIVE
```

Listing 6.2: Using SEND as a Table Name.

This means that **SEND** and **RECEIVE** only work as Service Broker commands when they are the first word in a command. The easiest way to ensure this is to put the semi-colon character (;) at the end of the previous line.

Message Bodies

The message_body of a Service Broker queue is a **varbinary(MAX)** column. This means a message body is up to two gigabytes of binary data. Most SQL Server datatypes can be cast to or from **varbinary(MAX)**, so you can send almost anything you want as a Service Broker message. If 2 GB of data isn't enough, the in-order delivery of Service Broker conversations makes it easy to split a very large message into 2GB pieces and reassemble them at the destination.

Most messaging applications use XML as the message body to simplify processing and decrease coupling between services. The new SQL Server XML datatype converts implicitly to and from **varbinary(MAX)**, so using Service Broker with the XML datatype is simple and straightforward.

The ordering assurances provided by Service Broker conversations also simplify message body handling. For example, SOAP-based applications have problems mixing binary and XML data in a single message. With a Service Broker conversation, an application can send an XML message followed by a binary message and be sure that the XML message will always be received first and that the binary message will never be received without the XML message. Sending different datatypes as separate, ordered messages simplifies the programming model for sending and receiving messages.

If you send a message with any datatype that can be cast to **varbinary(MAX)**, the **SEND** command does the cast for you. On the receiving side, you must know what kind of data the message contains so that you can cast the **varbinary(MAX)** message body to the correct type required for the application. Applications generally retrieve the message body as binary data and then process it based on the **message_type** value of the message.

If all the messages used by your application are XML, you can receive the messages directly as XML data.

Note:

Your application must always be prepared to receive an XML message body, because Service Broker error and control message bodies are XML. This generally means receiving the message body into a binary variable and then casting it to the correct type for the message type.

If your application uses a limited number of datatypes, you might want to handle the casting in the **RECEIVE** statement. In the example in Listing 6.3, the message will be returned in a varbinary or XML variable depending on the **message_type_name**.

```
DECLARE @ConversationHandle uniqueidentifier
DECLARE @MessageType sysname
DECLARE @XMLMessage xml
DECLARE @BinMessage varbinary(MAX);

RECEIVE TOP (1) @ConversationHandle = conversation_handle,
            @MessageType = message_type_name,
            @XMLMessage = CASE message_type_name
                    WHEN 'ISBNBinary'
                            THEN NULL
                    ELSE
                            message_body
                    END,
            @BinMessage = CASE message_type_name
                    WHEN 'ISBNBinary'
                            THEN message_body
                    ELSE
                            NULL
                    END
        FROM [ISBNLookupTargetQueue]
```

Listing 6.3: RECEIVE with Different Types of Message Bodies.

Transactions

Transactions are required for "exactly once," in-order message processing. To understand the reason for this, consider a messaging application that processes messages read from a file. The application reads a message, performs some processing (such as updating records in a database) and then removes the message from the file. If the application crashes after doing some work—but before removing the message from the file—the message will still be in the file when the application restarts and will be processed again. If the application tries to avoid this problem by removing the message from the file before processing it, there is the danger that a crash before the processing is complete will leave the message unprocessed and not in the file. This means that even though the message is only delivered once, it might be processed twice or not at all.

Transactional messaging solves this problem by wrapping the removal of the message from the queue and the processing of the message in the same transaction. If the application crashes, the queue and the database are both rolled back to the state they were in before the transaction started. The rollback also includes **SEND** commands. If processing a message involves sending messages to other services, transactional messaging will ensure that the messages aren't sent unless the transaction commits. This is easy for Service Broker, because sending a message just inserts it into the queue hidden table. Like any **INSERT**, the inserted row isn't visible until the transaction commits. If the transaction rolls back, the message is never visible in the queue.

Because message processing in Service Broker applications requires transactions, careful transaction design is an important factor in Service Broker application design. Transactions affect both the correctness and the performance of Service Broker applications.

Rolling back a transaction puts messages back on the queue for reprocessing. Because the rolled back messages will be processed again, the transaction must include all the database updates that were done as part of processing the message. The updates must be redone the next time the application processes the message.

Should multiple messages be included in the same transaction? It depends. In some cases, the number of writes that can be made to the transaction log is the limiting factor for performance, so more messages per transaction is a better answer. In other cases, the limiting factor is contention for locks held by other transactions, so smaller transactions are a better answer.

In general, you should receive and process all the messages available in a conversation group in a single transaction unless there is a good reason for the messages to be processed in separate transactions. This is generally safe in terms of lock contention because the messages in a conversation group are all related. Presumably they are all going after the same rows in the database and these rows are generally different than the rows accessed by other conversation groups. For example, if you are using a conversation group for all the messages related to a single sales order, much of the data accessed in processing that order won't overlap with other orders. Keeping the transaction active while processing all the related messages on the queue should not cause a lot of contention issues.

There are cases where it makes sense to process unrelated messages in a single transaction. The canonical examples of this are inserting order rows into an order history table or inserting rows in a log table. In this case, lock contention isn't an issue, so batching the messages into fairly large transactions would improve performance. You have to trade off the improved performance of larger batches against latency and error handling. The results of message processing aren't available until the transaction commits, so larger batches increase latency. One error in a batch of 10,000 messages rolls them all back and the whole batch has to be reprocessed.

Most of the Service Broker examples in this book show one message processed per transaction. This is to simplify the Service Broker logic and not bury it in complex flow control logic. You can use this pattern for simple, low-volume applications, but if you need maximum performance, you should consider ways to process multiple messages per transaction. However, this assumes processing a message is a quick operation. If each message kicks off 20 minutes of processing, the performance boost of processing multiple messages in a transaction is negligible. In general, you will have to benchmark to find the best transaction size for a given application.

The Receive Loop

Most Service Broker applications that receive and process messages are built around a simple receive loop. This loop starts by receiving one or more messages, processing the messages, sending zero or more messages, committing the transaction, and then starting again. There are many variations on this theme but the underlying structure is the same. The code snippet in Listing 6.4 shows the receive loop of a service that processes the ISBN lookup requests we saw in Chapter 1:

```
DECLARE  @MessageType sysname
DECLARE  @ConversationHandle uniqueidentifier
DECLARE  @MessageBody XML  --  Only XML messages in this
                               --  example


--  This procedure just sits in a loop processing messages from the
--  queue until the queue is empty
WHILE (1 = 1)  -- Nearly always true
BEGIN
   BEGIN TRANSACTION  -- Always use an explicit transaction
   -- Receive the next available message
   WAITFOR (
      RECEIVE top(1) -- just handle one message at a time
         @MessageType=message_type_name,
         @MessageBody=message_body,
         @ConversationHandle = conversation_handle
      FROM [ISBNLookupTargetQueue]
   ), TIMEOUT 5000
   -- If we didn't get anything after 5 seconds, the queue is
   -- empty so bail out
   if (@@ROWCOUNT = 0)
      BEGIN
         Rollback Transaction
         BREAK
      END
   ELSE
   -- Check for End Dialog Messages
   IF (@MessageType =
      'http://schemas.microsoft.com/SQL/ServiceBroker/EndDialog')
      BEGIN
         -- When we receive an End Dialog, we need to end also.
         End Conversation @ConversationHandle
      END
   ELSE
   -- Check for Error Messages
   IF (@MessageType =
```

```
          'http://schemas.microsoft.com/SQL/ServiceBroker/Error')
      BEGIN
      -- Handle the error here.  Maybe log it or send a notification
      -- to someone.  If there are still messages in the queue you
      -- may or may not want to process them.
      -- If work has already been done and committed as part of this
      -- dialog, you may have to issue compensating transactions to
      -- undo it.
      -- At this point the other end can't receive or send messages
      -- so once the error is handled the only thing to do is end
       -- our end of the dialog also.
       END Conversation @ConversationHandle
   END
   ELSE
   -- Check for Application Messages
   IF (@MessageType = 'ISBNLookupRequest')
       BEGIN
          SEND ON CONVERSATION @conversationHandle
              MESSAGE TYPE [ISBNLookupResponse]
              (N'<ISBNLookupResponse>
                 <Title>The Rational Guide to SQL Server Service Broker</Title>
              </ISBNLookupResponse>')

       -- End the conversation because we're done with it.
       END CONVERSATION @conversationHandle
   END -- process message
   COMMIT TRANSACTION
END -- while loop
```

Listing 6.4: Basic RECEIVE Loop.

Notice that the loop in Listing 6.4 only processes one message per transaction. (Chapter 7 will show an example of processing all the messages in a conversation group). Request-response services like this one that receive a message, return a single response, and end the conversation use this style of message loop. Because the application only receives one message on each dialog, the **RECEIVE TOP(1)** statement simplifies this case.

The pattern of receiving a message at the top of a loop and then executing conditional logic based on the type of message received is a very common one. In fact, those of you who have been around Windows programming awhile will recognize this style of message loop as the core of all Windows applications.

The first two message types processed in the loop shown in Listing 6.4 are **conversation error** messages and **end conversation** messages. You can receive these message types from any Service Broker queue, so your application must always include logic to handle them.

The Service Broker internal logic generates some of the error messages—for example, an XML message failing validation or a message sent to a service that doesn't exist. Applications may also generate error messages with an **END CONVERSATION WITH ERROR** command. See Books Online for more information about this command. Chapter 2 also covers the semantics of ending a dialog. Remember that both endpoints must end the conversation before the rows in sys.conversation_endpoints for the conversation will go away.

The rest of the conditional message processing statements must include logic to process all possible received message types for the queue. The query in Listing 6.5 will list all possible non-system types for a given queue:

```
select distinct T.name from
    sys.service_message_types T
    JOIN sys.service_contract_message_usages TC
        ON T.message_type_id = TC.message_type_id
    JOIN sys.service_contract_usages CS
        ON TC.service_contract_id = CS.service_contract_id
    JOIN sys.services S ON CS.service_id = S.service_id
    JOIN sys.service_queues Q ON S.service_queue_id = Q.object_id
    where Q.name = 'ISBNLookupTargetQueue'
```

Listing 6.5: Select All Possible Messages Types for a Queue.

This illustrates the value of Service Broker contracts. The message types received by a service are limited by the contracts it supports, so you know exactly what message types your application has to deal with.

Error Handling

Because Service Broker services usually run as background processes, handling errors is important. In an application with a UI you can just tell the user what's wrong and have them decide what to do about it. That doesn't work for background processes with no way to communicate with an interactive user.

SQL Server 2005 makes error handling easier with the **TRY–CATCH** commands. This allows you to group all your error handling logic in the catch block. In some simple applications, it might be possible to put the complete message processing logic into a single **TRY–CATCH** command, but it's usually a good practice to handle each message type in a separate **TRY–CATCH** command.

Transactions make error handling straightforward by allowing you to roll back all the work done in processing a message—including all sent and received messages. The key to making this work correctly is to only roll back transactions when reprocessing the message is likely to succeed. For example, a deadlock error should be retried because it will eventually succeed, but a primary key violation caused by trying to insert a record that already exists will retry forever.

If you decide to rollback a transaction, remember that everything is rolled back. Therefore, if you want to log the error to a log file, you have to do it after the rollback in a new transaction.

If you choose not to roll back the transaction, you have two alternatives:

▶ **END** the conversation with an error and commit the transaction. This is the normal way to handle permanent errors. In most cases, if one message in a conversation can't be processed, the whole conversation is unsalvageable. For example, if the conversation is entering a new book into our publishing system and finds there's another book with the same ISBN number, there's no point in going any further.

▶ **COMMIT** the **RECEIVE** command to remove the message from the queue but continue the conversation. This is only appropriate if the conversation can complete successfully without processing this message. A typical example might be an error that must be resolved manually but doesn't prevent the business transaction represented by the dialog from completing successfully. In this case, you must roll back the work that was done without rolling back the **RECEIVE** part of the transaction. The easiest way to do this is with a **SAVEPOINT**. The code snippet in Listing 6.6 shows how this works. After receiving a message, the **SAVE TRANSACTION** command establishes a **SAVEPOINT** so that the following work can be rolled back without rolling back the **RECEIVE** command. If processing the message fails with a transient error, the whole transaction (including the **RECEIVE** command) is rolled back. If the error is a permanent error such as a primary key constraint violation, the message is saved in a log table, the message processing is rolled back to the **SAVEPOINT**, and then the **RECEIVE** command part of the transaction is committed.

```
BEGIN TRANSACTION
RECEIVE top(1)
        @MessageType=message_type_name,
        @MessageBody=message_body,
        @ConversationHandle = conversation_handle
        FROM [ISBNLookupTargetQueue]
if (@@ROWCOUNT = 0)
        BEGIN
                ROLLBACK TRANSACTION
                BREAK
        END
-- Save the transaction
SAVE TRANSACTION AFTERREAD
        ...
        ...
        ...
IF (@MessageType = 'ISBNLookupRequest')
BEGIN
        BEGIN TRY
        ...
        ...
        ...
```

```
END TRY
BEGIN CATCH
        -- Check for transient errors.  The numbers depend
        -- on what you're doing
        IF error_number() IN
                (580,596,601,701,708,802,844,845,
                846, 847, 921,922, 923, 1121, 2502, 3967,
                3984, 3985, 1205, 2755, 3635, 3928, 17884,
                1203, 1221, 1807, 6292, 20041  )
        BEGIN
                ROLLBACK TRANSACTION
                CONTINUE
        END
        ELSE BEGIN
        -- Not a transient error.  Commit read.
                ROLLBACK TRANSACTION AFTERREAD
                INSERT INTO err VALUES (getdate(),
                        error_number(), error_message())
        END
    END CATCH
END -- PROCESS MESSAGE
COMMIT TRANSACTION
```

Listing 6.6: Handling Errors.

Conversation Timers

Service Broker includes another unique feature to make building asynchronous applications easy—the *conversation timer*. A conversation timer puts a message on the queue of the service that sets the timer when the time expires. In essence, it's like sending a message to yourself that will arrive at a specified time in the future.

The code sample in Listing 6.7 begins a dialog, sets a conversation timer on that dialog for 10 seconds, commits the transaction, and then waits for the message to be received when the timer expires.

```
DECLARE @ConversationHandle uniqueidentifier
BEGIN TRANSACTION
BEGIN DIALOG  @conversationHandle
    FROM SERVICE      [ISBNLookupResponseService]
    TO SERVICE        'ISBNLookupRequestService'
    ON CONTRACT       [ISBNBinaryContract];
BEGIN CONVERSATION TIMER ( @ConversationHandle ) TIMEOUT = 10;
COMMIT;
WAITFOR(RECEIVE * FROM [ISBNLookupinitiatorQueue])
```

Listing 6.7: Setting and Waiting for a Conversation Timer.

Note that the message arrives on the initiator queue when the conversation timer was set on the initiator side of the dialog. When you begin a conversation timer from the target side of the dialog, the message arrives on the target queue. There are actually two conversation timers for a conversation—one for each endpoint. The type of the message that arrives when the timer expires is http://schemas.microsoft.com/SQL/ServiceBroker/ DialogTimer.

A conversation timer is a unique kind of timer because it is persistent, and the delivery of the timeout message is transactional. This means that no matter how many times the application crashes or the database is restarted between when the timer is set and when it expires, the timer will deliver the timeout message. It also means that if there's a failure while the timer message is being processed, the transaction will roll back and the timer message will be delivered again. In high-availability applications, if the database fails over, the timer will also fail over to the backup database. You can even move the database to another SQL Server instance without losing the timer.

A very common pattern in asynchronous applications is for an application to send a message to another service to be processed and then go on to do other things, assuming that when the service is done, a response will come back. But what happens if no response is returned because the requested service is unavailable? If the conversation was started with a timeout value, it will eventually time out and return an error. In some cases, however, the conversation timeout may be set to several days or even years. Also, a conversation timeout ends the conversation with an error, which can be a very bad thing if a lot of work has taken place on the conversation. In these cases, setting a conversation timer to time out in a reasonable time will alert the sending application that something is wrong and allow it to handle the timeout without ending the conversation.

An important thing to keep in mind is that the conversation timer doesn't do anything beyond putting a message on the queue when the timeout expires. What the application decides to do when that message arrives is totally dependant on the application. Also notice that the **DialogTimer** message has a sequence number of **-2**, which means that it is received ahead of any other messages already in the queue when it arrives. We will see the conversation timer again in later chapters because it's a key part of many Service Broker applications.

Summary

The chapter explained how to use the **SEND** and **RECEIVE** commands to transfer data between Service Broker applications. In the following chapters we will cover the rest of the Service Broker API.

FREE

Bonus:

The following bonus material is available for free downloading when you register your book at www.rationalpress.com **(see the last page in this book for instructions):**

▶ Sample code for the examples in this book

▶ Bonus Chapter: "Troubleshooting and Administration"

Chapter 7

State Handling

We learned in Chapter 2 that Service Broker conversations can be long-running dialogs that last for days or months. It would obviously be incredibly inefficient and probably impossible to keep a copy of the application active for every active conversation. Service Broker applications, like most highly scaleable applications, solve this problem by maintaining persistent state between messages.

The state of an application contains enough information to pick up processing when the next message arrives. For example, the state for a book publishing application might track the status of each chapter in the book and the schedule for each book, so that when a chapter arrives from an author, reviewer, or editor, the application knows how to handle it. When a message arrives, the application retrieves the current state of the book, processes the message, and modifies the saved state to reflect the changes that processing the message caused.

Those of you who write Web applications or Web services have been told many times that state is evil and you should avoid maintaining state between messages if at all possible. However, if your application is running in the database, storing a little extra data in the form of application state doesn't impact scalability that much. The messaging operations, database updates, and state updates are all part of a simple single-phase transaction and are committed with the same log write. If your application runs outside of the database, consider how much state you're sending back and forth. Saving the "original request" message in the database might not be a big deal, but moving it back and forth to an external application every time a message comes in might be.

Using the Conversation Group ID as a State Key

Chapter 3 explained that dialogs related to a single business operation (like processing an order or publishing a book) can be grouped together into a conversation group to simplify message processing. All messages in the same conversation group contain the same conversation group ID, so this ID is a handy key for the state associated with the operation. Each message will contain the key for the state tables, which makes it simple to retrieve and restore the state.

Service Broker doesn't store application state for you. It just maintains a uniqueidentifier in every message that makes a handy key for whatever state tables your application wants to store. As an added bonus, there's a lock associated with the conversation group, so that if the state is only updated while processing messages, you don't have to worry about conflicting updates to the state. The rows in the state table aren't actually locked, but if the application only updates the state while it holds the conversation group lock, only one application thread at a time can update the state.

Retrieving State and Messages in a Single Round Trip

If you implement your application logic as a stored procedure, you can retrieve state whenever you need it. However, if your application logic connects to the database over a network connection, retrieving messages and state in a single round trip can significantly improve performance.

Service Broker includes the **GET CONVERSATION GROUP** command to make state retrieval easier. This command locks the first conversation group with messages on the queue and returns the conversation group id. You can then select the state from the state tables and receive the messages. Use the code shown in Listing 7.1 in a batch from a client application or in a stored procedure to retrieve both messages and state in a single round trip from the client to the database.

```
DECLARE          @ConversationGroup uniqueidentifier;

BEGIN DIALOG

GET CONVERSATION GROUP @ConversationGroup
        FROM [ISBNLookupTargetQueue];

SELECT ISBN, CreditCheckStatus, InventoryStatus, ShippingStatus
        FROM OrderState WHERE ConversationGroup = @ConversationGroup;

RECEIVE message_type_name, cast(message_body as XML),
conversation_handle
        FROM [ISBNLookupTargetQueue]
        WHERE conversation_group_id = @ConversationGroup;
```

Listing 7.1: Retrieving State Before the RECEIVE Command.

Notice that the **RECEIVE** statement uses the conversation group ID in a **WHERE** clause. This is necessary to ensure that the messages are received from the conversation group that the state is associated with. Otherwise, you may retrieve messages for a different conversation group and the state won't match the message.

The Receive Loop with State

Retrieving and updating state changes the basic receive loop we encountered in Chapter 6 into two nested loops. The outer loop uses the **GET CONVERSATION GROUP** command to start a transaction, lock a conversation group, and retrieve the state. The inner loop then receives all the messages available in the conversation group one at a time. The inner loop ensures that all the messages on the queue associated with the state row are processed before the outer loop retrieves another state row. Once all the messages in the queue from that conversation group are processed, the state is updated with any data that has changed while processing the messages, and the transaction is committed. This works well if there are a limited number of messages from the conversation group on the queue. In applications where a continuous stream of messages arrives on the same conversation group (sales from a cash register or status from a manufacturing machine, for example) you should consider committing the transaction after a number of messages so that the transactions don't get too big. Listing 7.2 illustrates this 'loop within a loop' pattern for handling conversation groups that maintain state.

```
DECLARE         @ConversationGroup uniqueidentifier
DECLARE         @ISBN nvarchar(30)
DECLARE         @CreditCheckStatus int
DECLARE         @InventoryStatus int
DECLARE         @ShippingStatus int

WHILE (1 = 1)
BEGIN
        BEGIN TRANSACTION
        -- Find and lock a conversation group with messages to process
        WAITFOR (
                GET CONVERSATION GROUP @ConversationGroup
                        FROM [ISBNLookupTargetQueue]
        ), TIMEOUT 5000
        IF (@@ROWCOUNT = 0)
        BEGIN
                Rollback Transaction
                BREAK
        END
        -- Get the state for this conversation group
        SELECT @ISBN = ISBN, @CreditCheckStatus = CreditCheckStatus,
           @InventoryStatus = InventoryStatus,
           @ShippingStatus = ShippingStatus
           FROM OrderState WHERE ConversationGroup = @ConversationGroup
        IF (@@ROWCOUNT = 0)
        BEGIN
                SELECT @ISBN = '',@CreditCheckStatus=0,
                  @InventoryStatus=0,@ShippingStatus=0
                INSERT INTO OrderState VALUES
                  (@ConversationGroup, '', 0, 0, 0)
        END
        DECLARE         @MessageType sysname
        DECLARE         @ConversationHandle uniqueidentifier
        DECLARE         @MessageBody XML
        -- Inner loop to process messages in this conversation group
        WHILE (1 = 1)
        BEGIN
```

```
-- Receive the next available message in the conversation group
        WAITFOR (
                RECEIVE TOP(1)
                        @MessageType=message_type_name,
                        @MessageBody=message_body,
                        @ConversationHandle = conversation_handle
                        FROM [ISBNLookupTargetQueue]
                        WHERE conversation_group_id =
                                @ConversationGroup
        ), TIMEOUT 5
        IF (@@ROWCOUNT = 0)
        BEGIN
                BREAK
        END
        IF (@MessageType =
        'http://schemas.microsoft.com/SQL/ServiceBroker/EndDialog')
        BEGIN
                END CONVERSATION @ConversationHandle
        END     ELSE
        IF (@MessageType =
                'http://schemas.microsoft.com/SQL/ServiceBroker/Error')
        BEGIN
                --Handle Errors
                END CONVERSATION @ConversationHandle
        END     ELSE
        IF (@MessageType = 'ISBNLookupRequest')
        BEGIN
                -- Process the message
                SELECT @MessageBody
        END
END - Inner Loop
-- Update the state
UPDATE OrderState SET ISBN = @ISBN,
  CreditCheckStatus = @CreditCheckStatus,
  InventoryStatus = @InventoryStatus,
  ShippingStatus = @ShippingStatus
```

```
        WHERE ConversationGroup = @ConversationGroup
    COMMIT TRANSACTION
END    -- Outer Loop
```

Listing 7.2: A Basic RECEIVE Loop with State.

Now that you understand how to retrieve and update state data, the next logical question is what to store. The simple answer is that you should store enough data to resume the conversation when the next message arrives. This generally includes identification information such as the order number, part number, or ISBN number that the conversation is processing. The current state of the business transaction is also a good thing to keep. For example, "credit checked OK," "inventory allocated," or "parts on order." Conversation handles might also be important to maintain as state. If the conversation group is processing an order that arrived as a Service Broker message, the conversation handle to send the order status back to may be valuable state. Finally, if the conversation is managing a long-running business transaction, you should save information about what database updates were made while processing the conversation, in case an error or cancellation forces the application to undo the updates. For example, an order cancellation would result in deleting the order header and order lines, canceling a bill, stopping a shipment, restocking inventory, and so on.

Summary

Many applications need to maintain state information between conversation messages, because many related messages are used in a single business process. Service Broker doesn't store state information for you, but the conversation group ID included with every message can be an effective key for state information.

Chapter 8

Poison Message Handling

What Is a Poison Message?

All transactional messaging systems have to deal with *poison messages*, which are messages that cannot be processed by the destination service. When the transaction processing a message encounters an error and rolls back, the **RECEIVE** statement rolls back so that the message is still on the queue. This is a good thing if the transaction succeeds the next time the message is processed. However, in some cases no amount of reprocessing will make the transaction succeed, and the message will be reprocessed forever. For example, if processing a message inserts a row into a table that already contains a row with the same primary key, the transaction will fail forever unless the duplicate row in the table is deleted.

The term "poison message" often gives the impression that these messages are sent as a malicious attack on the application. While that's possible, the majority of poison messages are the result of application errors or invalid data. A poorly written query or incorrect data entry causes more poison message issues than hacker attacks.

Defensive Coding

The first line of defense in handling poison messages is writing the message handling code so that messages that will never be successfully processed aren't rolled back. We discussed this pattern in Chapter 6. In some cases, it makes sense to roll back to a savepoint just after the **RECEIVE** command and commit the **RECEIVE** command to get the message out of the queue and allow the conversation to continue. This strategy requires that the conversation finish successfully without processing a message. This may be correct for some messages, but in most cases the messages are sent as part of the same conversation (because the business transaction required them to be processed in order), so skipping a message invalidates the whole dialog. In that case, ending the conversation with an error is a more appropriate strategy.

Careful coding is always the best approach to handling poison messages, because only the application knows whether it makes sense to roll back a transaction and try the receive statement again. We will see in the next section that Service Broker provides a fallback method of handling poison messages, but writing your application to prevent poison messages puts you in control of how they are handled.

Last Resort Protection

Service Broker includes a mechanism for detecting and dealing with poison messages. When a queue experiences five rollbacks in a row, Service Broker disables the queue and raises a SQL Server event. An application that subscribes to the poison message event notification with the **CREATE EVENT NOTIFICATION** command can either try to automatically resolve the poison message or notify an administrator who can manually resolve the poison message and re-enable the queue. (See Listing 8.2 for an example of how to subscribe to the poison message event.) The following SQL statement will display a 0 in the *is_receive_enabled* column for any queues that have been disabled:

```
SELECT name, is_receive_enabled FROM sys.service_queues
```

The Service Broker poison message handler is different than most messaging systems. Other messaging systems move poison messages they find to a dead-letter queue and go on to process the rest of the messages in the queue. This approach won't work for Service Broker dialogs, because dialog messages must be processed in order. Skipping a poison message violates the dialog semantics.

While Service Broker effectively detects poison messages, disabling the queue temporarily halts all processing for applications associated with the queue. For this reason, good defensive coding techniques should be used to prevent poison messages in the first place.

To see how this works, we will create stored procedures to simulate a poison message. The first procedure (*SendaMessage*) sends a message to the **ISBNLookupTargetQueue**. The second procedure (*RollbackAll*) receives this message and rolls back the transaction. This is repeated until the queue is disabled. At that point, the **RECEIVE** statement will fail because the queue is disabled and the stored procedure will exit (see Listing 8.1).

```
CREATE PROCEDURE SendaMessage AS
DECLARE @ConversationHandle uniqueidentifier
BEGIN TRANSACTION
BEGIN DIALOG  @conversationHandle
    FROM SERVICE     [ISBNLookupResponseService]
    TO SERVICE       'ISBNLookupRequestService'
    ON CONTRACT      [ISBNLookupContract];
SEND ON CONVERSATION @ConversationHandle
   MESSAGE TYPE [ISBNLookupRequest]
   (N'This is a poison message');
COMMIT
go
CREATE PROCEDURE RollbackAll as

DECLARE        @MessageType sysname
DECLARE        @ConversationHandle uniqueidentifier
DECLARE        @MessageBody varbinary(MAX)
-- Enable the queue so we can run this more than once
-- After running this the poison message handling will
-- diable the queue.
ALTER QUEUE ISBNLOOKUPTARGETQUEUE WITH STATUS = ON
WHILE (1 = 1)
BEGIN
        BEGIN TRANSACTION
        WAITFOR (
                RECEIVE top(1)
```

```
                        @MessageType=message_type_name,
                        @MessageBody=message_body,
                        @ConversationHandle = conversation_handle
                        FROM [ISBNLookupTargetQueue]
        ), TIMEOUT 500
        if (@@ROWCOUNT = 0)
                BEGIN
                        ROLLBACK TRANSACTION
                        BREAK
                END
        -- just to a rollback no matter what we receive to simulate a poison
➲message
        print 'rollback'
        ROLLBACK TRANSACTION
END -- while loop
Go
```

Listing 8.1: Poison Message Example.

The following procedures will create a poison message.

1. Make sure the queue is enabled by typing the following code:

    ```
    SELECT name, is_receive_enabled FROM sys.service_queues
    ```

2. Simulate a poison message by typing the following code:

    ```
    EXEC SendaMessage
    go ·
    EXEC RollbackAll
    go
    ```

3. Check the queue status again by typing the following code:

    ```
    SELECT name, is_receive_enabled FROM sys.service_queues
    ```

As you can see, receiving a poison message disables the queue and causes all **RECEIVE** statements from that queue to fail. While this keeps the poison message from tying up the application, it also stops all work on the queue. To resolve this situation, you must either **RECEIVE** and **COMMIT** the poison message or **END** the conversation that contains the poison message. Stop all applications reading from the queue, enable the queue and execute a **RECEIVE** from the queue. This will retrieve the message from the top of the queue, which is the one causing the problem. Either commit the **RECEIVE** command if the dialog can safely continue without this message or **END** the dialog. Examining the SQL Server error log file for what was causing the message to fail and rollback will help you determine how to handle the message. This assumes that only one message is processed at a time by the application. If this isn't the case, the poison message could be any of the messages in the same conversation group as the message at the top of the queue.

You will want to know when a poison message causes a queue to be disabled so that you can deal with it promptly. Use an event notification to do this. The script in Listing 8.2 will register an event notification for the **ISBNLookupTargetQueue** poison message detection.

```
CREATE QUEUE PoisonMessageNotifyQueue;
GO
CREATE SERVICE PoisonMessageNotifyService ON QUEUE PoisonMessageNotifyQueue
([http://schemas.microsoft.com/SQL/Notifications/PostEventNotification]);
GO
CREATE EVENT NOTIFICATION ISBNPoisonMessage ON QUEUE ISBNLOOKUPTARGETQUEUE
FOR Broker_Queue_Disabled
TO SERVICE PoisonMessageNotifyService, 'current database' ;
```

Listing 8.2: Subscribing to the Poison Message Event.

When a poison message is detected on the **ISBNLookupTargetQueue**, an event notification message will be put on the **PoisonMessageNotifyQueue** that we just created. Run the poison message procedures to try this out. You should see a message with a message body that looks like the one in Listing 8.3:

```
<EVENT_INSTANCE>
  <EventType>BROKER_QUEUE_DISABLED</EventType>
  <PostTime>2005-02-10T09:59:34.153</PostTime>
  <SPID>20</SPID>
  <DatabaseID>7</DatabaseID>
  <TransactionID />
  <NTUserName />
  <NTDomainName />
  <HostName />
  <ClientProcessID />
  <ApplicationName />
  <StartTime>2005-02-10T09:59:34.140</StartTime>
  <ObjectID>2073058421</ObjectID>
  <ServerName>Test03</ServerName>
  <LoginSid>AQ==</LoginSid>
  <EventSequence>2745</EventSequence>
  <IsSystem>1</IsSystem>
</EVENT_INSTANCE>
```

Listing 8.3: Poison Message Notification Message.

To see which queue this event was sent from, first find out the name of the database corresponding to the `<DatabaseID>7</DatabaseID>` element:

```
SELECT name, database_id FROM sys.databases WHERE database_id = 7
```

Use that database and then get the queue name corresponding to the `<ObjectID>2073058421</ObjectID>` element:

```
SELECT name, object_id FROM sys.service_queues
WHERE object_id = 2073058421
```

You can do whatever makes sense with the notification messages. The procedure in Listing 8.4 will send an e-mail with the contents of the message body.

```
CREATE PROCEDURE HandlePoisonMessageEvents as
declare        @MessageType sysname
declare        @ConversationHandle uniqueidentifier
declare        @MessageBody XML
while (1 = 1)
begin
        begin transaction
        WAITFOR (
                RECEIVE top(1)
                        @MessageType=message_type_name,
                        @MessageBody=message_body,
                        @ConversationHandle = conversation_handle
                        FROM PoisonMessageNotifyQueue
        ), TIMEOUT 5000
        if (@@ROWCOUNT = 0)
                BEGIN
                        Rollback Transaction
                        BREAK
                END
        IF (@MessageType = 'http://schemas.microsoft.com/SQL/Notifications/
⮑EventNotification')
        begin
                declare @cmd nvarchar(MAX)
                SET @cmd = 'dbo.sp_send_dbmail
                @profile_name = ''AdventureWorks Administrator'',
                @recipients = ''danw@Adventure-Works.com'',
                @body = ''' + CAST(@MessageBody as nvarchar(MAX)) + '',
                @subject = ''Poison Message Detected'' ;'
                EXEC (@cmd)
        end -- process message
        commit transaction
end -- while loop
go
```

```
ALTER QUEUE PoisonMessageNotifyQueue WITH
ACTIVATION (
    STATUS = ON,
    PROCEDURE_NAME = HandlePoisonMessageEvents ,
    MAX_QUEUE_READERS = 1 ,
    EXECUTE AS SELF )
```

Listing 8.4: Handling the Poison Message Event.

Summary

Any message that contains data that can force the message processing transaction to roll back can become a poison message. If left unhandled, a poison message will be processed over and over in an infinite loop. The correct way to avoid poison messages is to code your application to handle errors without producing poison messages. If one slips through, Service Broker will detect the repeated rollbacks and disable the queue to keep a poorly handled message from becoming a poison message.

Chapter 9

Activation

We learned in Chapter 6 that the **RECEIVE** command pulls messages from Service Broker queues for processing. This means that when messages arrive on a queue, an application must be running to process them.

There are many ways to ensure that a Service Broker application is available to process messages when they arrive. External applications can be run as Windows Services or started by the Windows scheduler. Stored procedures can run as startup procedures, as SQL Server agent jobs, or as activated procedures.

Traditionally, messaging applications handled queues by continuously polling the queue to see if any messages had arrived or by using a trigger on the queue that would start the receiving application every time a message arrived on the queue. The first approach wastes a lot of resources when there are few messages arriving on the queue, and the second approach wastes a lot of resources on starting the application if messages are arriving at a high rate. Service Broker activation takes the best feature of both approaches. When a message arrives on a queue, a stored procedure is started to process it only if there isn't already a stored procedure running to process it. When a stored procedure is started, it keeps receiving messages until the queue is empty. This means resources aren't wasted by polling an empty queue and resources aren't wasted starting an application to process each message that arrives.

What is Activation?

Service Broker *activation* is a unique way to ensure that the right resources are available to process Service Broker messages as they arrive on a queue. To use activation, you associate a stored procedure with a queue. The stored procedure must receive and process messages from the queue it is associated with. The **receive message** loops described in Chapters 6 and 7 work well in activated stored procedures.

When a queue has an activation procedure defined and a message arrives on that queue, some special logic in the commit process (which writes the message row into the transaction log) checks to see if there is a copy of the activation procedure running. If there isn't a stored procedure running to receive messages from the queue, the activation logic starts one. A well-behaved procedure receives and processes messages from the queue until the queue is empty and then exits. Because the stored procedure only starts when there isn't one running already, activation is more efficient than message triggers that fire for every message that arrives.

When the activation logic finds that a stored procedure is running already, it also checks the number of arriving messages against the number of processed messages to determine whether the activated stored procedure is keeping up with the incoming message rate. If the incoming message rate is higher than the processing rate, another copy of the stored procedure is started. This continues until either the activated stored procedures are able to keep up with the incoming rate or until a configured maximum number of copies have been started. The right number of resources is always available to process messages in a queue because activation starts more procedures when the load increases, and the stored procedures exit when the queue is empty.

Some messaging systems offer triggers that fire when a message arrives. This is not as efficient as activation because the messaging processing logic has to handle the trigger and then receive the message as each message arrives. Activation only gets involved when the first message arrives or when the receivers aren't keeping up. As long as messages are arriving often enough that the **RECEIVE** statement doesn't time out, activation doesn't do anything.

After hearing about Service Broker activation, many people mistakenly assume that activation is required for Service Broker applications. It is not. Activation is a tool to make it easier to write services that execute as stored procedures, but there are a variety of equally valid ways to execute Service Broker services.

Configuring Activation

Activation is configured through the **CREATE QUEUE** or **ALTER QUEUE** statements. Listing 9.1 shows a typical example of configuring activation:

```
ALTER QUEUE [ISBNLookupTargetQueue]
   WITH ACTIVATION (
        STATUS = ON,
        PROCEDURE_NAME = [ProcessLookup] ,
        MAX_QUEUE_READERS = 10,
        EXECUTE AS 'Larry' )
```

Listing 9.1: Configuring Activation.

In Listing 9.1, the **STATUS** parameter controls whether activation starts the stored procedure or not. You can set **STATUS** to **OFF** to temporarily stop activation while troubleshooting a problem or to reduce load during peak processing times by stopping non-critical processing. For example, if you are using a Service Broker service to populate a reporting database, you might want to use an agent job to stop activation of that service during peak processing times.

In Listing 9.1, **PROCEDURE_NAME** is the name of a stored procedure that receives and processes messages from the queue. Configuring a stored procedure for activation creates a queue monitor for the queue. When messages are added to the queue and after 15 seconds of inactivity, the queue monitor determines whether a stored procedure should be started. When stored procedures are started, they are owned by the queue monitor. If one of them throws an exception, the queue monitor will catch it and start a new copy. The queue monitor also makes sure that the activated procedure is well-behaved. For example, if an activated procedure never receives any messages, no more copies will be started.

You can see all the queue monitors configured in a SQL Server instance by running this query:

```
SELECT * FROM sys.dm_broker_queue_monitors
```

To determine which queue monitor corresponds to a particular queue, get the database_id from the **sys.databases** view and the queue_id from the **sys.service_queues** view.

To find out what activated procedures are running in an instance, execute the following query:

```
SELECT * FROM sys.dm_broker_activated_tasks
```

The **MAX_QUEUE_READERS** parameter defines the maximum number of stored procedures that the queue monitor will start to service this queue. This parameter limits the amount of system resources that will be used to service this queue. Setting **MAX_QUEUE_READERS** to too large a value will not cause problems unless the volume of messages on the queue is causing other database activity to lose performance.

Too small a value for the **MAX_QUEUE_READERS** parameter will cause increased latency for messages processed by this queue because they will have to wait until a procedure is available to process them. If the messages aren't time critical and resources are tight, this is probably an acceptable situation. If message latency is becoming an issue, try monitoring the **sys.dm_broker_queue_monitors** view when latency is unacceptable. If the number of tasks is consistently at the maximum, try using the **ALTER QUEUE** command to increase **MAX_QUEUE_READERS**. This parameter change will take effect immediately, so you should be able to determine if adding more queue readers solves the problem.

There are two other factors to consider in the performance of activated stored procedures:

► Activation will never start more queue readers than the number of conversation groups active on the queue. This is because the messages in a conversation group are processed serially (due to the conversation group lock), so if a queue contains 1000 messages in the same conversation group, they will be processed one at a time because of the conversation group lock. There is no reason to have more than one queue reader running in this case.

▶ The value of the **WAITFOR** timeout in the receive loop determines how long the queue must be empty before an activated stored procedure goes away. If the timeout is very long, activated procedures will linger a long time after they are no longer needed. On the other hand, if the timeout is too short, activated procedures will disappear during brief lulls in message traffic. If restarting the procedure is expensive, this will lead to poor performance. If the activation procedure is a small TSQL procedure, a timeout of 2-3 seconds is probably sufficient. If it is a large CLR procedure, 20-30 seconds may be more appropriate. The correct value depends on how long it takes to start a new procedure and how much variation exists in message arrival rates, so this value may take some tuning to get right. In general, if resources aren't extremely tight on the system, a little too long is better than a little too short.

The **EXECUTE AS** parameter defines which user context the activated procedure runs in. The queue monitors execute on background threads, so without the **EXECUTE AS** parameter, the activated procedure would run as the System Adminstrator. There are options to make the procedure execute as the queue owner or queue creator, but it is a good practice to specify the user by name so that it's obvious what context will be used. Be sure that the user you specify has **RECEIVE** permissions on the queue and **EXECUTE** permissions on the stored procedure (plus any other permissions required to process the messages received from the queue). The user specified in the **ALTER QUEUE** in Listing 9.1 was created using the following script:

```
CREATE LOGIN ActiveLogin WITH PASSWORD = 'akemssi>/2*7'
CREATE USER ActiveUser FOR LOGIN ActiveLogin
GRANT RECEIVE ON [ISBNLookupTargetQueue] TO ActiveUser
GRANT EXECUTE ON [ProcessLookup] TO ActiveUser
```

Tech Tip:
Because activated procedures run on background threads, there is no user connection on which they can report errors. Therefore, any error or PRINT output for an activated procedure is written to the SQL Server error log (ERROR.LOG). If activation doesn't appear to be working, your first move should be to check the error log for any error messages. Missing RECEIVE or EXECUTE permissions are two of the most commons causes of failure.

External Activation

Since activation only works for stored procedures, a frequent question is how to activate a queue reader that runs as a Windows process. In many cases, this isn't really an issue because external processes take a long time to start up and connect to the database, so running the external process as a Windows service or a startup task is the best solution. In cases where the message arrival rate varies significantly over time, there may also be performance advantages to starting and stopping external processes in response to changes in message activity.

The current Service Broker release doesn't include an external activator, but it does include hooks for use by an external activator and an example implementation you can use to build your own. The hooks for external activation are implemented as a SQL Server event notification. If you subscribe to the **QUEUE_ACTIVATION** event, an event will be fired whenever Service Broker activation would have started a new copy of the activation procedure. As luck would have it, event subscriptions use Service Broker services, so you already know most of what you need to know to subscribe to an event. The message type and contract for event notifications are system objects that are created when a database is created, so all you have to define to receive event notification messages is a queue and a service.

To set up the **ISBNLookupTargetQueue** to generate **QUEUE_ACTIVATION** event messages, run the script shown in Listing 9.2:

```
ALTER QUEUE [ISBNLookupTargetQueue]
    WITH ACTIVATION ( DROP )
CREATE QUEUE [PublisherEventQueue]
CREATE SERVICE [PublisherEventService] ON QUEUE [PublisherEventQueue]
([http://schemas.microsoft.com/SQL/Notifications/PostEventNotification])
CREATE EVENT NOTIFICATION PublisherActivationEvent
ON  QUEUE [ISBNLookupTargetQueue] FOR QUEUE_ACTIVATION
TO SERVICE [PublisherEventService];
```

Listing 9.2: Configuring the Activation Event for a Queue.

Notice that the first statement drops activation on the queue. You can't use both internal and external activation on the same queue. Next, a queue and a service to receive the event messages are created. Finally, a **CREATE EVENT NOTIFICATION** command is used to subscribe to **QUEUE_ACTIVATION** events.

To test the activation event, send some messages to the **ISBNLookupRequestService**. When the first message arrives on **ISBNLookupTargetQueue**, activation will put an event notification message in **PublisherEventQueue**. The message body will resemble the one in Listing 9.3:

```
<EVENT_INSTANCE>
  <EventType>QUEUE_ACTIVATION</EventType>
  <PostTime>2004-12-22T21:06:20.790</PostTime>
  <SPID>30</SPID>
  <ServerName>PULISHER</ServerName>
  <LoginName>LookupLogin</LoginName>
  <UserName>LookupUser</UserName>
  <DatabaseName>PublisherDB</DatabaseName>
  <SchemaName>dbo</SchemaName>
  <ObjectName>ISBNLookupTargetQueue</ObjectName>
  <ObjectType>QUEUE</ObjectType>
</EVENT_INSTANCE>
```

Listing 9.3: Event Notification Message.

What you do with this message is up to you. There is an External Activator sample available in the Got Dot Net Code Gallery at http://www.gotdotnet.com/codegallery/codegallery.aspx?id=9f7ae2af-31aa-44dd-9ee8-6b6b6d3d6319. The sample external activator maintains a list of which tasks to execute for each queue in each database. A Windows service connects to the database and receives messages from the Event Notification queue. For each message received, the service starts the configured task to process messages. The assumption is that the task will open a connection to the specified database and receive and process messages from the specified queue until the queue is empty and then terminate. The external activation service keeps a persistent record of tasks and their process numbers to enable it to recover from failures. You can use the basic infrastructure provided in the SQL Server 2005 sample to implement a message processing infrastructure that suits your application needs.

Summary

Service Broker activation starts stored procedures to process messages on a queue. The activation algorithm controls the number of stored procedures receiving messages, so that the required number of resources are always available to process messages arriving on the queue. Service Broker in SQL Server 2005 includes internal activation to process messages with stored procedures, and also an event that can be used to extend activation to external processes.

Communications

Chapter 10

Service Broker Communications

Service Broker is often described as a platform for building reliable, asynchronous, distributed database applications. The previous chapters talked about reliable, asynchronous database applications, while this chapter and the following one will cover how to make these applications distributed. This chapter explains how Service Broker reliably sends messages between servers, and the next chapter explains how Service Broker sends messages securely.

Service Broker uses standard TCP/IP connections to send messages between SQL Server instances. Like many reliable messaging systems, the Service Broker communications protocol is a proprietary protocol optimized for efficient, reliable delivery of dialog messages. The communications system is designed to support other communication protocols, so it's likely that future releases will support Web Services protocols.

Service Broker Endpoints

In order for a remote system to open a TCP/IP connection to Service Broker, the Service Broker service must be listening on a TCP/IP port for incoming connections. You configure the port for Service Broker to listen on by creating an endpoint object. SQL Server 2005 uses endpoints to configure all incoming connection points, including TransactSQL, Service Broker, Database Mirroring, and HTTP.

When SQL Server 2005 is installed, only the default TDS endpoints are created, to limit the network surface area exposed. To create a listener for any other feature, use the **CREATE ENDPOINT** command. The following command will create a simple Service Broker endpoint:

```
CREATE ENDPOINT MainSSBEndpoint
AS TCP (
 LISTENER_PORT = 4025)
FOR SERVICE_BROKER (
  AUTHENTICATION = WINDOWS)
```

This creates a Service Broker endpoint that listens for connections on TCP/IP port 4025 and uses Windows authentication to establish the connection. Chapter 11 explains the authentication options available for Service Broker endpoints.

The port number can be any available port above 1024. Use **netstat −a** in a cmd window to see which ports are already in use. I don't generally recommend using 4022 (the Service Broker default port), because there is less chance of confusion if you have to consciously decide which port to use. If you have multiple SQL Server instances installed on a server and they all use port 4022, the first one to come up will grab the port and the rest will fail with an error in the SQL error log.

Only one Service Broker endpoint is currently supported per SQL Server instance, so attempting to create a second one will result in an error. Future versions of Service Broker may support listening on multiple ports to support more complex network configurations. In the first release, however, simplicity won out over flexibility.

To see the configuration of the Service Broker endpoint for your SQL Server instance, run the following commands:

```
SELECT * FROM sys.endpoints
SELECT * FROM sys.tcp_endpoints
SELECT * FROM sys.service_broker_endpoints
```

There are several more options for the TCP and SERVICE_BROKER clauses in the command. We will cover the forwarding options later in this chapter. For other options, refer to Books Online.

Broker Protocols

There are multiple protocols involved in a Service Broker conversation. At the high level, there is the dialog protocol (also called the endpoint protocol), which handles the exchange of messages between two dialog endpoints. This protocol manages message ordering, reliable delivery, dialog-level authentication and encryption, and dialog lifetime. There are often hundreds of dialogs open between any two Service Brokers even though only a few of these are sending or receiving messages at any given instant.

The lower level protocol is called the Adjacent Broker Protocol (ABP). The ABP manages the TCP/IP connection between two Service Brokers. An Adjacent Broker Protocol connection multiplexes messages from many dialogs. As we will see when we discuss forwarding later in the chapter, a message between two dialog endpoints might traverse several Adjacent Broker connections as it is routed to its final destination.

One way to understand the difference between the two protocols is to compare it to the way the telephone network works. At the high level, you make a phone call from your phone to another phone. You and the person at the other endpoint then carry on a conversation. At the low level, hundreds or thousands of these conversations travel over a single wire or fiber. In the same way, many Service Broker conversations can be multiplexed over a single TCP/IP connection between two SQL Server instances.

Sending a Message

This section follows a message from a sending application to a receiving application on another server. The journey starts when the sending application issues a **SEND** command. Service Broker's classifier logic uses the information in the **conversation_endpoints** table and the **routes** table to determine what to do with the message. If the destination for this message is a queue in the same SQL Server instance as the source, and if the queue is ready to receive messages, the message is inserted into the destination queue; otherwise, it is inserted into the **sys.transmission_queue** of the sending database. If the **RETENTION** option is set on the sending services' queue, the message is also copied to the sending queue. See the "Basic Routing" section later in this chapter for information on how the **routes** table is used by the classifier.

If the destination was a local queue, we're done with the **SEND** when the transaction commits. Otherwise, the message is committed into the **sys.transmission_queue**. A reference to the message is placed on an instance-wide list of messages to be sent. This global list ensures fairness in message dispatching across all the databases in the SQL Server instance. Message sending order is independent of which transmission queue they come from.

Dialog messages routed to the same network address are assembled into transport messages to be sent over an Adjacent Broker connection to the remote Service Broker. For efficiency, Service Broker sends multiple dialog message fragments with each socket call when possible. This is known as "boxcarring." Before it is sent, each message is signed to prevent alterations in transit and optionally encrypted.

Service Broker also fragments large messages. This keeps a single large message from tying up all the available bandwidth for the amount of time it takes to transfer the contents to the network. Fragmentation allows messages from other dialogs to be interleaved with fragments of a large message.

If a connection is open to the remote destination, the assembled boxcar is sent. If there isn't a connection available, a connection is opened and authenticated, (see Chapter 11 for more information on Adjacent Broker authentication). While the Adjacent Broker logic is waiting for the send to complete, another boxcar is assembled. This means an Adjacent Broker connection can effectively use all the bandwidth available. For this reason, only one connection is maintained between any two Adjacent Brokers.

Opening an Adjacent Broker connection can be relatively expensive, because several messages are exchanged to create and authenticate the connection. For this reason, connections are kept open for up to 90 seconds of idle time. As long as there is never a gap of over 90 seconds between messages, the connection will stay open.

When the message is received at the destination, the signature is checked and the message is decrypted if necessary. The classifier is called again to determine which queue the message should be inserted into. The **sys.routes** table in the **msdb** database is used for messages arriving from the network. If the message is bound for a queue in this instance, it is inserted into the queue. To maximize efficiency, several inserts are grouped into a single transaction if there are messages available.

Once the received message is successfully inserted into the queue, an *acknowledgement message* (ACK) is sent to the sender. The ack can either be included in the header of another message that is returning on the same dialog, or it can be a separate message. An ACK message can acknowledge several messages or message fragments with a single message. To maximize the possibility that the ACK will be returned as part of a normal dialog message and that it will acknowledge more than one message or fragment, the Service Broker receive logic waits for up to a second before acknowledging the message. This delay doesn't increase latency, because the message has already been successfully delivered. The delay just means the message will stay on the transmission queue in the sender a while longer.

When the ACK message is received at the sender, the message status is marked as successfully sent and the message is deleted from the **sys.transmission_queue**.

If the Adjacent Broker logic has problems either sending the message or opening a connection, the **transmission_status** column of the **sys.transmission_queue** will contain information about the error.

If an acknowledgement message for a message or fragment isn't received within the retry timeout, the message is sent again. The retry timeout starts at four seconds and doubles after each retry until it reaches a maximum of 64 seconds. This means that messages aren't retried too often if the sends fail multiple times. It also means that when the destination server comes back online after a failure, it can take up to a minute for some of the messages to be resent. Messages that arrive at the destination in a bad state—corrupted, incomplete, or with invalid credentials—are dropped by the destination and resent by the sender. There are SQL Trace events available in the Broker events that you can use to find out why messages are dropped at the destination. If Service Broker drops the message, it doesn't return an error back to the message sender. Monitoring the dropped message trace is the only way to find out that messages are being dropped.

Basic Routing

A Service Broker *route* maps a service to a destination where messages to that service should be sent. As discussed in the previous section, the Service Broker classifier uses this routing information to decide what to do with messages.

There are four routes involved in successfully delivering a message to its destination:

1. When the **SEND** command is executed, a route from the local **sys.routes** table is used to determine where the message is sent.

2. When the message arrives at the destination SQL Server instance, a route from the **sys.routes** table in the **msdb** database is used to determine which database will receive the message. This step is necessary because the same service may be defined in more than one database in the destination instance. Once the message has been successfully committed in the proper queue in the destination database, an acknowledgement is sent back to the sender–either as part of the header of a dialog message or as a separate message.

3. A route from the **sys.routes** table in the destination database is used to determine where to send the acknowledgement message. This is an important concept to understand. One of the most common configuration issues that Service Broker novices encounter is forgetting this return route. If you forget the return route, messages are delivered successfully to the destination queue, but they are never acknowledged. Messages stay in the **sys.transmission_queue** on the sending side and are resent periodically forever (or until someone adds the route at the destination, whichever comes first). If you notice successfully delivered messages still sitting in the sys.transmission_queue, or if you run Profiler on the destination server and see a bunch of messages being dropped because they are duplicates, check the route back to the sending service in the destination database.

4. When the acknowledgement message arrives at the sender's SQL Server instance, a route in the **msdb** database is used to route the message to the sending service's queue in the sending database.

These same four routes are used whether the message is sent from the initiator of the dialog to the target or from the target to the initiator. This explanation assumes that the sender and receiver make a direct connection between Service Broker endpoints. In some cases a message may be routed through multiple service brokers to reach its destination. See the "Forwarding" section later in this chapter for more information on the routes required for that scenario.

I often hear comments on the complexity of routing configuration. For example, the sender obviously knows where the message came from so why is a return route required? Also, why is the route used for every message? Once the first message is sent successfully, why not just keep track of the addresses in the dialog endpoint? The answer to these questions is that dialogs can last for days, months, or years—so there's a good chance that the addresses may change over the life of a dialog. Checking the route for every message means that if the route changes, the messages automatically start going to the new destination. A dialog that starts between Purchasing in Cleveland and Printing in Detroit may someday be between Purchasing in Denver and Printing in Singapore. Service Broker routing makes this possible without the applications even being aware that anything moved.

Creating Routes

Service Broker routes are SQL Server metadata objects created with a DDL command. A simple **CREATE ROUTE** statement looks like this:

```
CREATE ROUTE PrintingRoute
    WITH  SERVICE_NAME = 'Printing',
    ADDRESS =  N'TCP://printingserver:5743'
```

This route is named **PrintingRoute**. The name is used to refer to this route in **ALTER ROUTE** or **DROP ROUTE** commands. It has no other significance.

The **SERVICE_NAME** parameter is the name of the service for which this route provides routing information. It is the name that shows up in the **sys.services** view in the remote database and also the name of the **TO SERVICE** used in the **BEGIN DIALOG** command. Service names use binary collation regardless of the database collation, so the name in the **CREATE ROUTE** parameter must match the **BEGIN DIALOG** service name exactly. Using the wrong case for the name is a common source of errors.

The **ADDRESS** parameter indicates where the message should be sent. With a couple exceptions we'll cover next, the address is the network address and port of the SQL Server instance where you want to send the message. Note that this might not be the address of the final destination. If you use forwarding, this is the address of the next hop on the route to the final destination. This version of Service Broker only supports TCP/IP transports, so the network address must always begin with **TCP://**. The server can be a DNS name or an IP address as show below.

```
CREATE ROUTE PrintingRoute
  WITH SERVICE_NAME = 'Printing',
  ADDRESS = N'TCP://135.246.79.810:5743'
```

The port number must match the port number in the Service Broker endpoint of the SQL Server instance where messages for this service should be sent. If there is more than one SQL Server instance on the destination machine, the port number will indicate which instance to send the messages to.

Broker Instance

There are many scenarios where you may want to have the same service installed on many servers:

▶ Development, test, and production versions of the service.

▶ Load balancing. If Service Broker finds multiple routes to the same service name in the **sys.routes** table it will randomly pick one. This is a simple, reliable way to distribute processing across several copies of the same service.

▶ Partitioned Services. A service may be partitioned across multiple databases (customers A-M and N-Z, east coast shipments and west coast shipments).

In these cases, the **SERVICE_NAME** parameter isn't enough to determine which instance of the service you want to talk to. One possibility is to use different service names (such as CustomerA-M and CustomerN-Z), but that doesn't work in a load-balanced scenario. To resolve this ambiguity, Service Broker provides the **BROKER_INSTANCE** parameter. The **BROKER_INSTANCE** is a uniqueidentifier that identifies the service broker in a particular database. Even though the **BROKER_INSTANCE** identifier is currently a uniqueidentifier, it is specified as a string in case some future implementation requires some other format for the **BROKER_INSTANCE** identifier. To find the broker identifier for a database, use this query:

```
SELECT name, service_broker_guid FROM sys.databases
```

Keep in mind that the **BROKER_INSTANCE** identifier is the GUID of the database that you are sending messages to, not the database where the route is located. Here's a command to create a route with a broker identifier:

```
CREATE ROUTE ISBNRoute
WITH
    SERVICE_NAME = 'ISBNLookupRequestService',
    BROKER_INSTANCE = N'df5ccf83-fc74-401e-8bda-bbc2df315c39' ,
    ADDRESS = N'TCP://printingserver:5743'
```

Once you have created a route with **BROKER_INSTANCE** specified, you can use the instance identifier in the **BEGIN DIALOG** command to indicate which service you wish to open a dialog with:

```
BEGIN DIALOG  @conversationHandle
    FROM SERVICE      [ISBNLookupResponseService]
    TO SERVICE        'ISBNLookupRequestService',
                      ' df5ccf83-fc74-401e-8bda-bbc2df315c39'
    ON CONTRACT       [ISBNLookupContract];
```

Wild Card Routes

We have learned that Service Broker uses a combination of the service name and broker identifier to select the route to use for a message. If the classifier can't find an exact match for the service name and broker identifier specified in the **BEGIN DIALOG** command, it will look for a wildcard route. A route with no broker instance specified will match any broker instance and a route with no service name specified will match any service name.

Special Addresses

There are two addresses that have special meaning for Service Broker routes. When the route for a service name has an address of **LOCAL**, the classifier will look for the service name in the local instance to find which queue to put the message in. The first priority is the database where the route is located. If the service isn't found there, the classifier checks the services list, which contains all the services available in the local SQL Server instance. This command creates a local route:

```
CREATE ROUTE PrintingRoute
WITH SERVICE_NAME = 'Printing',
    ADDRESS = N'LOCAL'
```

One possible unforeseen consequence of using a local route is that if the service isn't found in the current database and is available in more than one other database in the instance, the classifier sees this as a load balancing situation and randomly picks one of the services as the target of the dialog. This usually isn't what the application intends and can lead to strange behavior. To avoid this, I recommend using a route with a **BROKER_INSTANCE** parameter to ensure that the dialog target is the database you intend. Because this is a common issue, Service Broker will implicitly route local dialogs that have a **BROKER_INSTANCE** parameter to the specified database even if there isn't a route specified for the target service.

If you look in the **sys.routes** view of a newly created database, you will find a route called **AutoCreatedLocal**. This route has no service name or broker identifier and an address of LOCAL. This route is the one we have used in all the examples so far. Because it is a wild card route, the classifier uses this route for any service name that doesn't have another route available. This is why we haven't had to create routes for any of the examples we have used so far—the **AutoCreatedLocal** route was sufficient because the examples all sent messages to local services. While this route makes developing simple applications easy, I recommend dropping it when deploying a distributed application in production. Without a wildcard route, you can be sure that messages only go where you intend them to go.

I am often asked "If a Service Broker application has several hundred dialog initiators opening dialogs with the same target, does the target need to have routes back to all the initiators?" The short answer is yes. Fortunately, Service Broker has a way to make a single route work for all the return messages. This shortcut is the **TRANSPORT** address. If the classifier finds a wildcard route with a **TRANSPORT** address after failing to find a more specific route, it will try to use the service name from the dialog as an address.

This is a difficult concept so let's use an example to explain it. Consider a scenario in which several publishers send manuscripts to the same printer for printing. The printer implements a *PrintingService* that accepts documents to print. The publisher then opens a dialog with the *PrintingService* to manage the printing process. In this example, the publisher's application runs on a server called **mannpub7** and the endpoint for the application's SQL Server instance listens on port 4067.

The publisher's application would include this service:

```
CREATE QUEUE [PrintResponseQueue]
CREATE SERVICE [TCP://mannpub7:4067/PubResponse]
ON QUEUE [PrintResponseQueue]
```

To open a dialog with the PrinterService, the publisher's application would make this call:

```
BEGIN DIALOG  @conversationHandle
    FROM SERVICE    [TCP://mannpub7:4067/PubResponse]
    TO SERVICE      'PrintingService'
    ON CONTRACT     [PrintContract];
```

The printing application would include this route in the database where the *PrintingService* is implemented:

```
CREATE ROUTE TransportRoute WITH ADDRESS = N'TRANSPORT'
```

When the *PrintingService* needs to send a response message on the dialog, the classifier will look for a route for a service called **TCP://mannpub7:4067/PubResponse**. If it doesn't find one, it will find the wildcard route with the **TRANSPORT** address and attempt to open a connection to **TCP://mannpub7:4067**. In our example, this will succeed and the message will be returned successfully.

A transport route can also be used in the **TO SERVICE** of a **BEGIN DIALOG**. This allows ad-hoc connections to services without creating the routing infrastructure normally required. The biggest disadvantage of using transport routes is that the address is embedded in the service name, so the service can't be moved to another server without destroying all existing dialogs to the service.

A Routing Example

To tie this all together, we will work through setting up the routes for a sample dialog. A dialog is established between two endpoints, so we will have to create two endpoints and four routes. The scenario for this example is an **EditingService** establishing a dialog with a *ProofreadingService* to transfer book chapters back and forth. The *EditingService* is located on a server named **MannEditing6** in a database named **EditDB** and the *ProofreadingService* is on a server named **MannProof4** in a database named **ProofDB**.

The DBA for **MannEditing6** runs the script shown in Listing 10.1.

```
-- Run on MannEditing6
CREATE ENDPOINT EditingEndpoint
AS TCP ( LISTENER_PORT = 4089)
FOR SERVICE_BROKER ( AUTHENTICATION = WINDOWS)

DECLARE @RemoteBrokerID uniqueidentifier
DECLARE @LocalBrokerID uniqueidentifier
DECLARE @cmd nvarchar(4000)

-- Get the Broker ID's
SELECT @RemoteBrokerID = service_broker_guid
        FROM MannProof4.master.sys.databases WHERE name = 'EditDB'
SELECT @LocalBrokerID = service_broker_guid
        FROM sys.databases WHERE name = 'msdb'

-- Create route for outbound messages
set @cmd = N'USE EditDB
CREATE ROUTE ProofRoute
WITH SERVICE_NAME = ''ProofreadingService'',
   BROKER_INSTANCE = ''' + CAST(@RemoteBrokerID as nvarchar(50)) + ''',
   ADDRESS = N''TCP://MannProof4:4743'''
exec (@cmd)

-- Create routefor inbound messages
set @cmd = N'USE msdb
CREATE ROUTE EditRoute
WITH SERVICE_NAME = ''EditingService'',
   BROKER_INSTANCE = ''' + CAST(@LocalBrokerID as nvarchar(50)) + ''',
   ADDRESS = N''LOCAL'''
exec (@cmd)
```

Listing 10.1: Setting Up MannEditing6 Routes.

The DBA for **MannProof4** runs the script in Listing 10.2.

```
-- Run on MannProof4
CREATE ENDPOINT ProofEndpoint
AS TCP ( LISTENER_PORT = 4743)
FOR SERVICE_BROKER ( AUTHENTICATION = WINDOWS)

DECLARE @RemoteBrokerID uniqueidentifier
DECLARE @LocalBrokerID uniqueidentifier
DECLARE @cmd nvarchar(4000)

-- Get the Broker ID's
SELECT @RemoteBrokerID = service_broker_guid
       FROM MannEditing6.master.sys.databases WHERE name = 'ProofDB'
SELECT @LocalBrokerID = service_broker_guid
       FROM sys.databases WHERE name = 'msdb'

-- Create route for outbound messages
set @cmd = N'USE ProofDB

CREATE ROUTE EditRoute
WITH SERVICE_NAME = ''EditingService'',
   BROKER_INSTANCE = ''' + CAST(@RemoteBrokerID as nvarchar(50)) + ''',
   ADDRESS =  N''TCP://MannEditing6:4089'''
exec (@cmd)

-- Create route for inbound messages
set @cmd = N'USE msdb
CREATE ROUTE ProofRoute
WITH SERVICE_NAME = ''ProofreadingService'',
   BROKER_INSTANCE = ''' + CAST(@LocalBrokerID as nvarchar(50)) + ''',
   ADDRESS =  N''LOCAL'''
exec (@cmd)
```

Listing 10.2: Setting Up MannProof4 Routes.

The **CREATE ROUTE** commands must be executed as dynamic SQL because the parameters must be literal strings. The **msdb** routes aren't strictly necessary because the **AutoCreatedLocal** route in **msdb** would route the messages correctly, but I generally use a specific route rather than relying on the wildcard routes. This removes any ambiguity in routing. Also, remember that the endpoint only needs to be created once on each SQL Server instance.

Routing and Database Mirroring

If the target of a route is a pair of databases connected through database mirroring, the address of the destination depends on which of the two databases is currently the primary database. To deal with this, a route to a mirrored pair of databases includes addresses for both of the databases in the pair:

```
CREATE ROUTE PrintingRoute
WITH SERVICE_NAME = 'PrintingService',
    BROKER_INSTANCE = N'df5ccf83-fc74-401e-8bda-bbc2df315c39' ,
    ADDRESS =  N'TCP://printingserver:5743',
    MIRROR_ADDRESS = 'TCP://printingserver2:5743' ;
```

When Service Broker sends a message on this route, connections to both addresses are opened and the message is sent to the primary database. If the primary database fails over, Service Broker detects this by subscribing to the Database Mirroring failover event, sending a message back to the sender, and immediately starting to send messages to the new primary database. This is a significant high-availability advantage for Service Broker, because the connection always sends messages to the current master with no impact to the sending application. Most other applications must detect the failure of the connection to the primary and then reopen their connection to the new primary. This can take a significant amount of time. Service Broker switches to the new primary in a few seconds.

Forwarding

There a several scenarios that require message forwarding in Service Broker networks. One is the case where two endpoints can't connect directly, so some kind of gateway is needed to connect the two endpoints. Another is when a large number of requesting services are all opening dialogs to the same service. In this case, the server hosting the service can become overextended by trying to handle a large number of connections in addition to servicing requests. One or more forwarders between the requesters and the service can handle the large number of connections and forward the messages to and from the service over a small number of connections (see Figure 10.1).

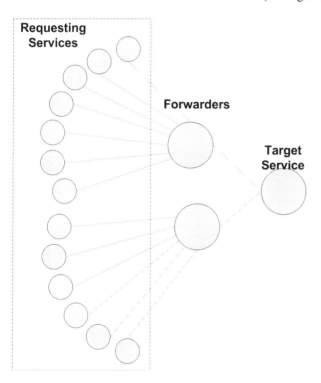

Figure 10.1: Forwarding Topology.

Before you can use Service Broker for forwarding, you must enable forwarding in the endpoint configuration:

```
ALTER ENDPOINT MainSSBEndpoint
FOR SERVICE_BROKER (
  MESSAGE_FORWARDING = ENABLED, MESSAGE_FORWARD_SIZE = 30)
```

This enables forwarding and also sets the maximum amount of memory to use for forwarding to 30 MB. Forwarded messages aren't persisted in the database. They are stored in memory until they are sent on to the next destination. If the maximum memory limit is reached, the oldest messages are discarded to make room. Remember that the message is saved in the sender's transmission queue until it is acknowledged, so it is safe to throw away a message from the forwarding buffer. When the retry timer on the sender expires, the message will be sent again, so there's no need to persist it at the forwarder.

Once forwarding is enabled, you have to populate the routing table in the **msdb** database. As we learned earlier, the routes in the **msdb** database are used to route incoming messages. If the **msdb** route specifies an external address, the incoming message is routed to the remote Service Broker.

For example, in our previous example of routes for dialogs between a publishing service and a printing service, you would insert a router between the two services by creating routes in the **msdb** database of the router, as shown in Listing 10.3:

```
CREATE ROUTE PrintingRoute
WITH
    SERVICE_NAME = 'Printing',
    BROKER_INSTANCE = N'df5ccf83-fc74-401e-8bda-bbc2df315c39' ,
    ADDRESS = N'TCP://printingserver:5743'

CREATE ROUTE PublisherRoute
WITH
    SERVICE_NAME = 'Publishing',
    ADDRESS = N'TCP://publishingserver:4041'
```

Listing 10.3: Forwarder Routes.

Once the forwarder is set up, the route in the publishing database is modified to point to the forwarder instead of the printing service, and the route in the printing database is modified to point to the forwarder instead of the publishing service.

Because forwarded messages are stored in memory, a forwarder can generally handle a higher message volume than a full Service Broker. In many cases, SQL Express will be adequate to handle message forwarding. Forwarding offers a lot of flexibility in Service Broker network configuration and using SQL Express as a forwarder makes it an economical choice.

Service Broker in SQL Server Express Edition

SQL Server Express Edition includes a fully functional Service Broker implementation. The only restriction is in the communication protocol. Somewhere in the route that a message takes between the dialog initiator and target, it must pass through a non-Express edition of SQL Server. For example, a SQL Express Edition database can open a dialog to a Standard edition database, a Standard edition database can open a dialog to a SQL Express edition database, or two SQL Express editions can talk through an Enterprise edition forwarder.

Service Broker in SQL Server Express also enables a variety of distributed messaging scenarios. Service Broker in a free database can be used in smart client applications to provide reliable, asynchronous, bidirectional communications. Because dialogs are bidirectional, a Service Broker service can send unsolicited messages to the client. These messages will be delivered reliably even if the client is offline when the message is sent. Other scenarios that require reliable message exchange in the face of system or network failures (such as point of sale terminals, ATM's, or manufacturing controllers) can also benefit from the reliable, persistent messaging offered by Service Broker. For more information on SQL Server Express, see *The Rational Guide to SQL Server 2005 Express*, available from www.rationalpress.com.

Summary

Service Broker includes a very sophisticated message transport and routing system based on a TCP/IP connection between SQL Server instances and a flexible message forwarding feature. The Service Broker reliable messaging protocol and routing features can be used to build large network infrastructures for the reliable delivery of Service Broker messages.

Did you know?

Database mirroring uses the Service Broker communication code for transferring database pages to the secondary database. Much of what you're learning about setting up Service Broker endpoints will apply when you set up database mirroring.

Chapter 11

Security

As you might expect with a feature that sends messages across the network, Service Broker has an extensive set of security options. As with most network products, security is the most complex and confusing part of configuring Service Broker, so this chapter explains each part of the security system in detail.

Keep in mind that not every Service Broker application requires all the security features we will cover. Simple applications that run within a single SQL Server instance require very little security configuration, applications that communicate within a secure LAN environment require a little more security and only applications that communicate across insecure WANs require the full set of Service Broker features. Even within an application you may decide that some dialogs should be encrypted and others don't need to be. Service Broker security is flexible enough to support all these options.

This chapter covers the individual security features of Service Broker and SQL Server 2005 and then discusses which features to use in which scenarios. But before we get into Service Broker security, we need to discuss certificates and keys.

Certificates

One of the new features of SQL Server 2005 is the ability to create and securely store certificates. Most modern distributed systems use certificates to establish user identity. If you have set up a secure Web site or Web services, you are probably familiar with certificate authorities and trust chains. Service Broker doesn't use the more esoteric features of certificates. As far as Service Broker is concerned, a certificate is a handy container for public-key/private-key pairs. We'll talk more about keys in the next section, but for now it's sufficient to know that a certificate contains a key and that the key can be used to prove who you are to a remote user.

For some scenarios, Service Broker uses certificates to authenticate the identity of the user who sent a message instead of using a password as most other SQL Server features do. To see why this is, imagine sending a Service Broker message to a remote service that might be down, or perhaps is a batch service that only runs at night. This is no problem for Service Broker because messages are persisted and reliably delivered. If Service Broker used passwords for dialog authentication, a dialog box would pop up requesting your password when the remote service started running at 3:00 A.M. You wouldn't have to get paged at 3:00 A.M. too many times before you were convinced that using certificates for dialog security is a good idea.

Public and Private Keys

Our normal experience with keys is that you use the same key to lock and unlock a lock. Public and private keys (also called asymmetric keys) are different: there are two keys and what you lock with one key can only be unlocked with the other. If I encrypt something with my private key, you can decrypt it with my public key. If you encrypt something with my public key, only I can decrypt it, because I'm the only one who has my private key.

This unique property of asymmetric keys can be used to establish a secure communications channel. I can send my public key out to you and anyone else who wants to send me data securely. You can then encrypt the data with my public key and send it to me, secure in the knowledge that only I can decrypt it because only I have the private key. If you send me your public key, I can in turn send you data that only you can decrypt. As long as we're both careful to be sure that our private keys remain secret, we can reliably establish each other's identity through the exchange of public keys.

The internet uses this basic scheme to build an elaborate identity system based on reliable third parties who distribute keys. Using certificate authorities, parties with no prior knowledge of each other can establish each other's identity by having the certificate authority vouch for the identity and the validity of the public keys they distribute. If I don't know who you are, I can still establish your identity with confidence by obtaining your public key from a third party we both trust—the certificate authority.

Service Broker doesn't get involved in these issues of trust. In order to establish identity, each endpoint must have the opposite endpoint's public key. Whether that public key is obtained from a certificate authority or exchanged on a floppy disk is a detail left up to the people deploying the system. You tell Service Broker which keys to use and Service Broker uses them to securely establish identity.

Symmetric Keys

Using asymmetric keys to reliably establish identity and encrypt messages works conceptually, but in reality, it's not practical. The reason is that using asymmetric keys to encrypt and decrypt data is *really slow*. Sending a few megabytes of data using asymmetric keys can take hours. On the other hand, symmetric key encryption and decryption is very fast.

A symmetric key works more like we expect a key to work—the same key both encrypts and decrypts the data. The disadvantage of symmetric keys is that both ends of the conversation must have the same key. Transferring a symmetric key between endpoints is risky, because if it's intercepted, a hacker can decrypt all the information sent using the key.

To get both the speed advantages of symmetric keys and the security of asymmetric keys, Service Broker uses asymmetric keys to securely exchange a symmetric key, which can then be used to encrypt the messages exchanged between two endpoints.

Service Broker Security

Now that you understand the basics of keys and encryption, we will discuss how these are used to secure Service Broker conversations. There are two distinct levels of security that Service Broker provides:

▶ **Transport security**—Secures the TCP/IP connection between two Service Brokers that are connected to the same network.

▶ **Dialog security**—Secures each individual dialog between the two dialog endpoints, regardless of how many networks the messages traverse as they travel between the conversation endpoints.

Transport security is easier to set up while dialog security is significantly more efficient in complex networks where messages traverse multiple forwarding Service Brokers. In some cases where the highest level of security is required, using both may be appropriate. After explaining how the two types of security work, we'll discuss which option should be used in your application.

Transport Security

Transport security secures the TCP/IP connection between two SQL Server instances on different servers. There are two parts to transport security :*authentication* (where the two endpoints determine that they are willing to talk), and *encryption* of the data on the wire. Authentication is required for all connections and encryption is optional. Both are configured as properties of the endpoint object through **CREATE ENDPOINT** or **ALTER ENDPOINT** statements.

Authentication

Service Broker offers two types of connection authentication: Windows and Certificate. Windows authentication uses the normal Windows authentication protocols—NTLM or Kerberos—to establish mutual authentication between the two endpoints of the connection. Certificate-based authentication uses the TLS authentication protocol (SSPI/SChannel) to authenticate the two endpoints. In general, Windows authentication should be used if both endpoints are in the same Windows domain and Certificate based authentication should be used if the endpoints are in different domains. These are recommendations, not rules. Consistency and ease of use are as important as technical considerations when deciding which method to use.

Windows Authentication

The following scripts demonstrate how to set up Windows authentication between two Service Broker endpoints. Figure 11.1 illustrates the network configuration. A SQL Server database on a server named **publisher03** is in communication with a SQL Server database on a server named **printer05** using Service Broker. We will create a Service Broker endpoint named **PublisherEndpoint** on **publisher05** and an endpoint named **PrinterEndpoint** on **printer03**. We will use Windows authentication to establish the identities of the servers when they connect.

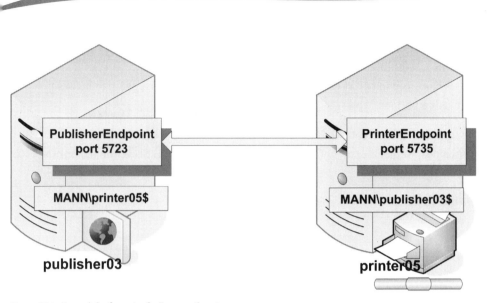

Figure 11.1: Network Configuration for Transport Security.

Start by creating the endpoint for **publisher03** by executing the following command:

```
CREATE ENDPOINT PublisherEndpoint STATE = STARTED
AS TCP ( LISTENER_PORT = 5723 )
FOR SERVICE_BROKER ( AUTHENTICATION = WINDOWS )
```

While still logged on to **publisher03**, create a SQL Server login that represents **printer05** in this database. If the SQL Server service account (the Windows user that the SQL Server service program runs as) is "local system" and both servers are in the "MANN" domain, then the login name is **MANN\printer05$**. Note that the only Kerberos authentication can use the machine account for authentication. If you network does not have Kerberos, you will need to either run the SQL Server instance with a domain user as the service account or use certificate authentication as described in the next section. If the SQL Server service account is a domain user, then the login name will be the name of that user—for example,**MANN\rwolter**. Notice that this login represents the service account of the remote SQL Server instance—not the service account of the instance where we are creating the connection endpoint. We authorize the remote SQL Server instance to connect to this endpoint by granting the login "connect" permissions on this endpoint. If this endpoint needs to connect to more than one remote Service Broker, you must create a login for each remote service account and grant each of them connect permissions to this endpoint. If you are trying to configure a large network, you may find it easier to configure all the SQL Server instances to use the same domain user as a Service Account. In this case, you may just configure all the endpoints to use Windows authentication and everything will just work.

For our example, create the login and grant connect permission with the following commands. Remember to do this while still logged on to SQL Server on the **publisher03** server.

```
CREATE LOGIN [MANN\printer05$] FROM Windows
GRANT CONNECT ON ENDPOINT::PublisherEndpoint to [MANN\printer05$]
```

You have now established one side on the authenticated connection. To establish the other side log on to the other SQL Server instance on **printer05** and create the endpoint with this command:

```
CREATE ENDPOINT PrinterEndpoint STATE = STARTED
AS TCP ( LISTENER_PORT = 5735 )
FOR SERVICE_BROKER ( AUTHENTICATION = WINDOWS )
```

When this is complete, create a login to represent **publisher03** using these commands:

```
CREATE LOGIN [MANN\publisher03$] FROM Windows
GRANT CONNECT ON ENDPOINT::PrinterEndpoint to [MANN\publisher03$]
```

You can now create a route in a database on each server and test the connection by sending a message. If the connection succeeds, the following command will return information about the connection:

```
select * from sys.dm_broker_connections
```

This connection will be shared by dialogs going in both directions between these two endpoints, so there should only be one connection between two endpoints.

If the connection fails, try the following:

1. Check the Windows event log on both machines for login errors.

2. Check the SQL Server error log for Service Broker errors.

3. Use profiler to look at "Audit Broker Login" and "Broker Connection" events.

To troubleshoot Kerberos issues, you can enable Kerberos logging on all the computers involved. See KB article 262177 for information on enabling Kerberos logging, at `http://support.microsoft.com/default.aspx?scid=kb;en-us;262177`.

This example used the default Windows authentication method, which first tries to authenticate using the Kerberos protocol. If Kerberos isn't available, it uses the Windows NTLM authentication protocol. You can force the authentication protocol to use only Kerberos or only NTLM if you prefer. See the **CREATE ENDPOINT** topic in Books Online for more information.

Certificate-Based Authentication

Windows authentication works well if both endpoints are in the same Windows domain. But if they are in different domains, Windows authentication can be complex and slow. In this case, you may choose to use the certificate-based authentication protocol. As we learned earlier, two systems can authenticate each other if each one has a certificate with its own private key and another certificate with the opposite endpoint's public key. Any data encrypted with the private key at one endpoint can only be decrypted with the corresponding public key at the opposite endpoint. This technique can be used by two endpoints to securely establish each other's identity. One endpoint encrypts some data with its private key and the opposite endpoint decrypts this data with the first endpoint's public key. If the data decrypts successfully, the decrypting endpoint knows that only the endpoint that owns the private key could have encrypted it. When this exchange happens in both directions, both endpoints can be sure that they are talking to the opposite endpoint they expect. The advantage of this method is that authentication only requires the certificates—there is no need for the endpoints to contact a domain controller as there is with Windows authentication.

Each endpoint requires two certificates for this key exchange to succeed—the endpoint's own private key and the public key corresponding to the opposite endpoint's private key. This is a total of fours keys—one public and one private at each endpoint. Figure 11.2 shows these four certificates and how they relate to the endpoint. The private key certificate is associated with the endpoint and the public key certificate is owned by a user that has CONNECT permission on the endpoint. If you want to allow any Service Broker to connect to this SQL Server instance, you can grant connect permission to "public." In this case, authentication between the two SQL Server instances will still be done, but if the authentication succeeds, the connection will be allowed unconditionally. This is useful when all the connecting machines are located in the same trusted network and network security will prevent connections from untrusted machines.

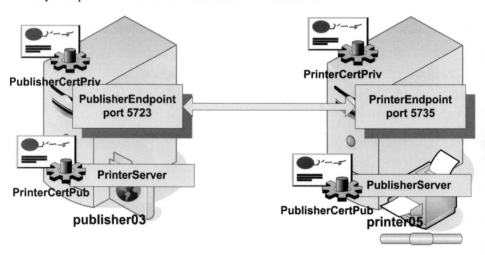

Figure 11.2: Network Configuration for Certificate Transport Security.

The next set of scripts shows how to set up certificate authentication for the two endpoints in this illustration. For simplicity, I am using certificates that SQL Server creates, but if your organization has other ways of creating and distributing certificates used for authentication, these certificates will work equally well. See the CREATE CERTIFICATE topic in Books Online for more information on creating different kinds of certificates and loading certificates from files.

The first thing we will do is create a certificate used to identify the PublisherEndpoint. I called this one **PublisherCertPriv** to indicate that it is a private key certificate. I didn't supply an ENCRYPTION_PASSWORD to encrypt the private key, so the private key will be encrypted with the database master key. This is required for certificates used for Service Broker authentication so Service Broker can get to the private key. After creating the certificate, it is backed up to a file called C:\PubCert. This file will be used to transfer the certificate to the opposite endpoint. The backup statement doesn't include a private key option, so only the public key is written to the file. The only parameter required for the certificate is **SUBJECT**. It doesn't matter what you specify for the subject, but make it something descriptive. Execute these commands from the master database:

```
CREATE CERTIFICATE PublisherCertPriv
      WITH SUBJECT = 'ForPublisherAuth'
BACKUP CERTIFICATE PublisherCertPriv TO FILE = 'C:\PubCert'
```

Now that the publisher's certificate exists, we can associate it with the PublisherEndpoint using the following command:

```
CREATE ENDPOINT PublisherEndpoint STATE = STARTED
AS TCP ( LISTENER_PORT = 5723 )
FOR SERVICE_BROKER ( AUTHENTICATION = CERTIFICATE PublisherCertPriv )
```

Now that the PublisherEndpoint exists and has a private key certificate to use to identify itself, we can do the same thing on the **printer05** machine, by typing this code:

```
CREATE CERTIFICATE PrinterCertPriv
      WITH SUBJECT = 'ForPrinterAuth'
BACKUP CERTIFICATE PrinterCertPriv TO FILE = 'C:\PrntCert'
```

And this:

```
CREATE ENDPOINT PrinterEndpoint STATE = STARTED
AS TCP ( LISTENER_PORT = 5723 )
FOR SERVICE_BROKER ( AUTHENTICATION = CERTIFICATE PrinterCertPriv )
```

Both endpoints now have Service Broker endpoint objects with private keys associated with them. We now have to introduce the endpoints to each other by exchanging public keys. The first step in this process is left as an exercise for the reader. The public key certificate files must be transported securely to the opposite system. As the name implies, a public key is 'public,' so it doesn't matter to whom you give it. But when you receive a public key, it is important that you get the right one. There's a whole certificate authority infrastructure that Web-based applications use to verify public keys, but for our purposes, secure e-mail or FTP are probably sufficient.

Once the certificates have been exchanged, all we have to do is associate them with a login that has **CONNECT** permissions for the endpoint. The following commands will do this.

On the **printer05** machine, execute the following commands:

```
CREATE LOGIN PublisherServer WITH PASSWORD = 'dj47dkri837&?>';
CREATE USER PublisherServer;
CREATE CERTIFICATE PublisherCertPub AUTHORIZATION PublisherServer
       FROM FILE = 'C:\PubCert';
GRANT CONNECT ON ENDPOINT::PrinterEndpoint to PublisherServer
```

This allows the **publisher03** endpoint to connect to the **printer05** endpoint. Next, execute these commands on the **publisher03** machine:

```
CREATE LOGIN PrinterServer WITH PASSWORD = 'l(j<7dksi6737&?>';
CREATE USER PrinterServer;
CREATE CERTIFICATE PrinterCertPub AUTHORIZATION PrinterServer
       FROM FILE = 'C:\PrntCert';
GRANT CONNECT ON ENDPOINT::PublisherEndpoint to PrinterServer
```

In many cases, you will want to connect to more than one other SQL Server instance. To enable these connections, simply exchange certificates and create logins for each remote machine you want to be able to connect to. All the connections will use the same local private key certificate associated with the endpoint, but will use different public key certificates associated with a login. To revoke a remote Service Broker's right to connect to your SQL Server instance, just drop the user or deny the login connection permission on the endpoint.

You can now create a route in a database on each server and test the connection by sending a message. If the connection succeeds, the following command will return information about the connection:

```
select * from sys.dm_broker_connections
```

This connection will be shared by dialogs going in both directions between these two endpoints, so there should only be one connection between two endpoints.

If the connection fails, try the following at both ends of the connection:

1. Check the SQL Server error log for Service Broker errors.

2. Use Profiler to look at "Audit Broker Login" and "Broker Connection" events.

The protocol that Service Broker uses to authenticate the endpoints with each other is the same SChannel protocol that the SSL uses when connecting secure Web pages. To troubleshoot SChannel issues, you can enable SChannel logging on all the computers involved. See KB article 260729 for information on how to enable SChannel logging: http://support.microsoft.com/default.aspx?scid=kb;en-us;260729.

By default, certificates expire and become unusable. In this example, we created certificates without specifying an expiration date. In this case, the expiration date is set to one year from when the certificate is created. If you want to specify a longer or shorter expiration period, the **CREATE CERTIFICATE** command has options for setting the expiration to a date of your choosing. When a certificate is about to expire, it must be replaced. In order to avoid disruption, you must do this in the correct order. If you change the certificate in the endpoint, all connections to endpoints that don't have the new certificate will fail to deliver messages. However, the dialog won't fail, so when the certificate is replaced it will continue from where it left off. To avoid this, create a new certificate and send the public key certificate to all remote connections. The remote Service Broker can associate this certificate with the user who represents the SQL Server instance whose certificate that will be changed (a user can be associated with multiple certificate by using the **AUTHORIZATION** clause in the **CREATE CERTIFICATE** command). Once all the remote endpoints have added the new certificate to their users, you can change the local endpoint to point to the new certificate by using the **ALTER ENDPOINT** command. Once the new certificate is being used by all endpoints, the old certificate can be dropped. This process can take a while, so don't wait until the certificate expires to start changing it.

Encryption

Authentication is required for all transport connections. Along with authentication, all transport messages are checksummed and signed to ensure that the messages are not altered during transport. Service Broker also encrypts messages to prevent them from being monitored, if desired. Message encryption is required by default so that the endpoints we configured in the previous sections will send all messages encrypted. Encryption imposes some processor overhead, so if Service Broker traffic is being sent over a trusted LAN connection where tight security is not required, you may want to turn encryption off to increase the efficiency of message transmission. To turn off encryption, you may set the **ENCRYPTION** attribute of the endpoint to **DISABLED** with the **CREATE ENDPOINT** or **ALTER ENDPOINT** commands. For example, to disable encryption on the **publisher03** to **printer05** connection you could use the following commands.

On **printer05**, you would execute:

```
ALTER ENDPOINT PrinterEndpoint STATE = STARTED
FOR SERVICE_BROKER ( AUTHENTICATION = WINDOWS, ENCRYPTION = DISABLED )
```

On **publisher03**, you would execute:

```
ALTER ENDPOINT PublisherEndpoint STATE = STARTED
FOR SERVICE_BROKER ( AUTHENTICATION = WINDOWS, ENCRYPTION = DISABLED )
```

There are three possible values for the **ENCRYPTION** attribute: **REQUIRED**, **SUPPORTED**, and **DISABLED**. These three values let the administrator set up a complex network where some connections use encryption and others don't—even when these connections use the same endpoint. Table 11.1 shows the possible combinations of encryption attribute values and whether data on the connection will be encrypted.

Endpoint A	Endpoint B	Encrypted?
REQUIRED	REQUIRED	YES
REQUIRED	SUPPORTED	YES
REQUIRED	DISABLED	ERROR
DISABLED	DISABLED	NO
DISABLED	SUPPORTED	NO
SUPPORTED	SUPPORTED	YES

Table 11.1: Encryption Attribute Values.

For example, suppose you have a connection from A to B and another one from B to C. If you want the A to B connection data encrypted and the B to C data unencrypted, you would set A to **REQUIRED**, B to **SUPPORTED**, and C to **DISABLED**.

Service Broker supports two different algorithms for encryption. The default algorithm is **RC4**. This is the more efficient algorithm, so normally you should stay with the default. If required, you can configure connections to use the **AES** algorithm. See Books Online for more information on setting the algorithms.

In general, the overhead of encrypting all the network traffic is high enough that you should look closely at whether or not to enable encryption on a connection. If your normal network security is adequate to protect Service Broker data or if the data isn't highly confidential, encryption probably shouldn't be used. Remember that authentication and signing of the data detects any data alterations on the network, so the only thing encryption adds is privacy. Many companies use VPNs or other techniques to protect network data. If the data is already protected by one of these means, Service Broker encryption is probably redundant. Remember that Service Broker defaults to the most secure options. You must consciously decide that the default settings provide more security than required and configure a less secure connection.

Dialog Security

So far we have learned about the security that Service Broker provides for data sent between two connected Service Broker endpoints. The options provided are adequate for most applications but for certain security requirements, some applications may need to use dialog security in addition to transport security. This section explains what dialog security is and when you should consider using it in addition to transport security.

As the name implies, dialog security is used to secure complete dialogs from the initiator of the dialog to the target of the dialog. The security features provided are similar to transport security—authentication, message integrity, and encryption. The difference is that this security works between dialog endpoints instead of between transport endpoints. This means that dialog messages that are routed through a complex network of Service Brokers to reach their final destination are encrypted at one of the dialog endpoints and decrypted at the other endpoint. Figure 11.3 illustrates this point. Messages traveling between the dialog initiator and the dialog target go through two forwarders. When dialog security is used, the messages going from the initiator to the target will be encrypted at the initiator and decrypted at the target. If transport security was used instead, the messages would be decrypted and re-encrypted at each forwarder, so the message would be encrypted and decrypted three times in route. The extra overhead can cause significant delays and increase processing loads.

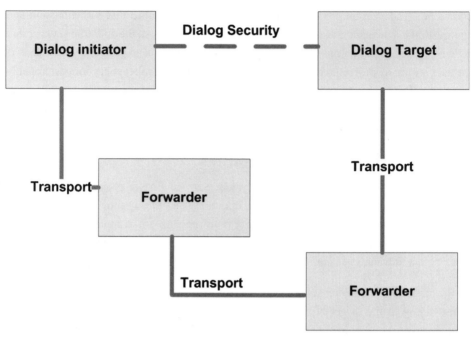

Figure 11.3: Forwarding Network.

Dialog security also provides authentication at the dialog level. This means that two services engaging in a dialog can reliably know that the service they are talking is exactly who they think it is. Authentication is a harder problem in asynchronous dialogs than it is with normal connection-oriented network protocols. Dialogs are persistent and can last through multiple database restarts, moving the database to a different server, failovers, and so on. Dialogs may last for years. Maintaining secure communications between dialog endpoints under these circumstances requires a different kind of security protocol.

Before getting into how to configure and manage dialog security, let's spend a little time understanding that basic security protocol. Dialog authentication uses certificates to authenticate the endpoints with each other. The way this works is a little different than the certificate-based authentication used by the Service Broker transport protocol. This difference is required because dialog endpoints are authenticated with each other once, and then this authentication lasts for the lifetime of the dialog. The asynchronous nature of dialogs also means that it's possible that the two services communicating over a dialog may never be running at the same time, so connection-oriented protocols won't work.

Dialog authentication requires a total of four certificates. Each Service has its own private key certificate and a certificate with the public key of the opposite Service. Because dialogs only exist between two endpoints, only these four certificates are required. The initiator of the dialog encrypts some data with its own private key and signs it with the target endpoint's public key. This encrypted data is sent to the target in the header of the first dialog message. When this message arrives at the target dialog endpoint, the public and private keys corresponding to the keys used to encrypt and sign the data are used to decrypt it. If it is decrypted successfully, the two endpoints have reliably established each other's identity, because only the four keys at these two endpoints could have successfully encrypted and decrypted the data.

As we learned earlier in the chapter, asymmetric key encryption and decryption are expensive operations. If they were used every time a dialog was established, the throughput of Service Broker would be reduced. To get around this problem, part of the data encrypted and decrypted during the authentication process is a symmetric key called the *Key Exchange Key* (KEK). Once the KEK has been reliably transferred between the initiator and target of the dialog, the two endpoints have a shared secret (the KEK) that only the two of them know. This shared KEK can then be used to transfer more data between the two endpoints. Successfully transferring this data can now be used to establish the identities of the endpoints, because only the endpoints sharing this symmetric key can successfully encrypt and decrypt the data. Using the KEK to establish authentication means that the asymmetric key encryption and decryption only need to be used when a new KEK must be exchanged. Because the KEK is cached in memory, the KEK must be re-established whenever the database is restarted. The KEK also expires periodically, and a new KEK is created and exchanged. The KEK is transferred with the first message of every dialog so that it is always available when required.

The data transferred with the KEK is the session key for the dialog. The session key is the symmetric key used to encrypt and sign every message sent on the dialog. The initiator generates a session key, encrypts it with the KEK and sends it to the target in the header of the first message. The target generates another session key and sends it back to the initiator in the header of the first message in that direction. We haven't discussed anonymous dialogs yet, but you should understand that an anonymous dialog uses the same session key in both directions.

To summarize what we have covered so far, the dialog initiator generates a KEK if there isn't already one available for the target and signs it with the initiator's private key. It then signs it with the target's public key. A session key is generated and encrypted with the KEK. The encrypted keys are copied into the header of the first message and cached locally. The KEK is stored in memory and never written to disk. The session key is encrypted with the database master key and stored in the conversation endpoint table. The KEK encrypted with the public and private keys is also cached in memory so that it can be used in other messages without redoing the asymmetric encryption. The message is then hashed, signed, encrypted with the session key, and then given to the transmission layer for transport to the target endpoint.

When the message arrives at the target endpoint, Service Broker checks its cache for the KEK used in the message. If it isn't cached already, the encrypted KEK from the message header is decrypted with the public key from the local certificate and cached in memory. The session key is decrypted with the KEK, stored in the conversation endpoint table and used to decrypt and verify the message contents. When the first message is sent back to the initiator, a new session key for the return direction is generated, encrypted with the KEK, and used to sign and encrypt the return message (there are minor exceptions to this for unsequenced messages and anonymous dialogs, but this is the general case). The initiator includes the security header with the keys in every message it sends until a message is received from the target. Once the first message is received from the target, the initiator can be sure that the target has the proper session key. The security header isn't sent in subsequent messages.

Messages include a timestamp and are valid for 30 seconds after they are sent. In reality, this time is 30 minutes and 30 seconds, because a 30 minute allowance for clock synchronization between the message sender and receiver is included in the timeout. Key Exchange Keys are valid for six hours from the time they are created.

Configuring Dialog Security

In the previous section, we learned that dialog security requires four certificates to secure a dialog—one public-key, private-key pair for each direction. In this section, we'll learn how to create the certificates and users required to make dialog security work.

Figure 11.4 illustrates the objects that must be created to configure dialog security. You may notice that this resembles the objects required for transport security. The main difference is that these certificates are associated with database users rather than logins.

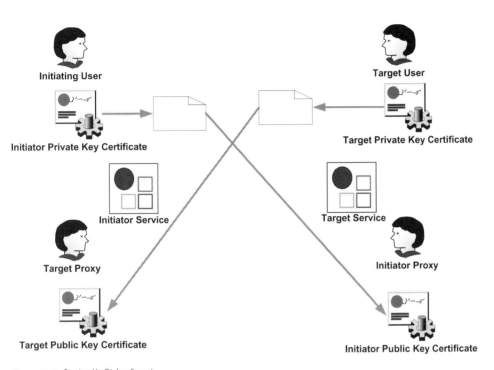

Figure 11.4: Setting Up Dialog Security.

To illustrate the commands required to configure dialog security, we will use a dialog that is opened between the **publisher03** PrintResponse Service and the **printer05** PrintManuscript service. The initiator runs on the **publisher03** server and the target runs on the **printer05** server.

Normally, security configuration starts at the target endpoint. The target is the endpoint that provides the service to one or more initiator endpoints. Normally, the target is set up once when the service is deployed and the initiator is set up on any databases that use the service supplied by the target.

The commands in Listing 11.1 are executed in the **Printer** database on the **printer05** server.

```
-- Create a user to represent the "PrintManuscript" Service
CREATE USER PrintManuscriptUser WITHOUT LOGIN
-- Grant control on the PrintManuscript service to this user
GRANT CONTROL ON SERVICE::PrintManuscript TO PrintManuscriptUser
-- Create a Private Key Certificate associated with this user
CREATE CERTIFICATE PrintManuscriptCertPriv
        AUTHORIZATION PrintManuscriptUser
        WITH SUBJECT = 'ForPrintManuscript'
-- Dump the public key cert to a file for use on the initiating server
BACKUP CERTIFICATE PrintManuscriptCertPriv
        TO FILE = 'C:\PrintManuscriptCertPub'
```

Listing 11.1: Configuring the Target Endpoint.

In Listing 11.1, the first command creates a database user to represent the PrintManuscript service. The user is created with no login so that the database can be moved between servers or duplicated without moving the logins between servers. While any user can be used here, a no-login user is easier to manage. The user must have CONTROL permission on the target service.

The next command creates a private key certificate that will be used to authenticate the service to initiators. This certificate must be owned by the user representing the target service. The last command dumps the public key part of the certificate to a file. This file will be used by initiators to authenticate the service. The next step in setting up security is to transfer this file to the initiator. The file only contains a public key, so it's not a disaster if it goes astray, but you must transfer it in a way that the initiator can be sure that it got the right certificate. In a local network, a shared directory is the simplest way to do this. Signed Email, FTP, thumb drives, and floppy disks will also work.

Once the public key certificate has been distributed reliably to the initiators, the commands in Listing 11.2 can be used to set up the security on the initiator side of the dialog.

```
-- Create a user to own the "PrintResponse" Service
CREATE USER PrintResponseUser WITHOUT LOGIN
-- Make this user the owner of the FROM service
ALTER AUTHORIZATION ON SERVICE::PrintResponse  TO PrintResponseUser
-- Create a Private Key Certificate associated with this user
CREATE CERTIFICATE PrinterResponseCertPriv
        AUTHORIZATION PrintResponseUser
        WITH SUBJECT = 'ForPrintResponse'
-- Dump the public key cert to a file for use on the printer05 server
BACKUP CERTIFICATE PrinterResponseCertPriv TO FILE = 'C:\Publisher03CertPub'
```

Listing 11.2: Configuring the Initiator Endpoint.

In Listing 11.2, the first two commands create a no-login user and make this user the owner of the **FROM SERVICE** of the dialog. Next, a private key certificate owned by this user is created. This certificate will represent the initiator in the authentication process. The last command dumps the certificate to a file so that it can represent the initiator on the target database to complete the authentication exchange.

Now that we have established the identity of the initiator, we can import the target's certificate to be able to authenticate the target. Use the commands shown in Listing 11.3.

```
-- Create a user to represent the "PrintManuscript" Service
CREATE USER PrintManuscriptUser WITHOUT LOGIN
-- Import the cert from the Printer owned by the user just created
CREATE CERTIFICATE PrintManuscriptCertPub
        AUTHORIZATION PrintManuscriptUser
        FROM FILE = 'C:\PrintManuscriptCertPub'
```

Listing 11.3: Importing the Target's Certificate.

These commands create a user to represent the target service and import the target service's certificate owned by the user we created. The next step is to identify which user the **BEGIN DIALOG** command will use to find the right certificate to use to authenticate with the target service. To do this, create a **REMOTE SERVICE BINDING** to bind the user we just created to the **TO SERVICE** used in the **BEGIN DIALOG** command:

```
CREATE REMOTE SERVICE BINDING ToPrintManuscript
        TO SERVICE 'PrintManuscript'
        WITH USER = PrintManuscriptUser
```

The **BEGIN DIALOG** command now knows which two certificates to use to authenticate the dialog—the private key certificate associated with the owner of the **FROM SERVICE**, and the certificate owned by the user bound to the **TO SERVICE** with the **REMOTE SERVICE BINDING**. These two certificates are used to create the security header sent with the first message of the dialog, as described above.

The last piece of the authentication puzzle is identifying the initiator to the target service. The target service controls which initiators have permission to begin dialogs to the service by granting permissions to the users associated with the initiator's public keys, as shown in Listing 11.4.

```
-- Create a user to represent the "Publisher03" Server
CREATE USER Publisher03User WITHOUT LOGIN
-- Import the cert from the Publisher owned by the user just created
CREATE CERTIFICATE Publisher03CertPub
        AUTHORIZATION Publisher03User
        FROM FILE = 'C:\Publisher03CertPub'
GRANT SEND ON SERVICE::PrintManuscript TO Publisher03User
```

Listing 11.4: Creating a User and Importing a Certificate.

The **Publisher03User** represents the initiator because it owns the certificate containing the initiator's public key. This user must have **SEND** permission on the target service to be able to put messages on the target service's queue. Each service that wants to call the target service must have a user and certificate to represent it installed in the target database. This allows the administrator of the target database to control which remote services have access to the services supplied by the target database.

Anonymous Services

If the target service is going to supply services to a large number of dialog initiators, importing the certificates and provisioning users for all the initiators can be a significant administrative burden. There are other scenarios where the target service wants to process requests from any initiator who makes the request without authenticating the initiator. To accommodate these scenarios, Service Broker includes an *anonymous dialog* feature. In an anonymous dialog, the target is authenticated to the initiator so that the initiator can be sure that its messages are being processed by the correct service, but the initiator isn't authenticated with the target.

To indicate to Service Broker that a dialog is anonymous, the **REMOTE SERVICE BINDING** is created with the **ANONYMOUS** option set to **ON**. The security header in the first message from the header is sent with only the target's public key. The owner of the **FROM SERVICE** does not need a private key certificate because it isn't used to authenticate the connection. On the target side, there is no need to create a user to own the initiator's public key certificate. One implication of this is that there is no user to grant **SEND** permission for the target service, because the target has no way to know which user sent the message. For this reason, **SEND** permission must be granted to **PUBLIC** for the target service when anonymous dialogs are used.

Use this command to create a **REMOTE SERVICE BINDING** for an anonymous dialog:

```
CREATE REMOTE SERVICE BINDING ToPrintManuscriptAnon
    TO SERVICE 'PrintManuscript'
    WITH USER = PrintManuscriptUser, ANONYMOUS = ON;
```

There is no need to send the initiator's public key to the target for anonymous dialogs, nor is there a need to create a user in the target database to represent the initiator. The only additional configuration required at the target endpoint is to grant **SEND** permission to **PUBLIC** in the target database:

```
GRANT SEND ON SERVICE::PrintManuscript TO public
```

Another distinguishing feature of anonymous dialogs is that the same session key is used to encrypt and sign traffic going in both directions. In general, use anonymous dialogs when the target service can complete a request securely without knowing the identity of the application requesting the service, or if identity will be established through another mechanism, such as a password or credit card number included in the message.

When to Use Security

By default, transport connections are authenticated, and all messages are encrypted and signed. Dialogs by default require security. This means that the default configuration provides the maximum protection for Service Broker messages. It also means that the default configuration settings require the maximum amount of configuring and consume the maximum amount of processor resources. While there are many situations that require this amount of security, some scenarios have less stringent security requirements, either because the data is not highly sensitive or because the network provides the required security. For example, if the network is an optical LAN in a secure computer room or a VPN, you may decide that the extra protection that Service Broker encryption provides isn't necessary.

This section explains how to reduce the default security levels to what is required for your configuration. Remember that too much security is a better problem to have than not enough security. When in doubt, err on the side of caution.

You may be wondering how all the examples we went through earlier worked with no security configuration. When both endpoints of a dialog are in the same SQL Server instance—either in the same database or in different databases in the same instance—encryption is never done. The Service Broker messages never leave the server's memory, so there's no reason to encrypt them. Permissions must be set up correctly, but encryption is not done and authentication is handled by the database. There are still two security issues you must deal with, however. If the dialogs are not created with the **ENCRYPTION** option set to **OFF**, there must be a master key created for the database. If the initiator and target of the dialog are in different databases in the same instance, you may have to set the **TRUSTWORTHY** bit on the **INITIATOR** side of the dialog (see the Note at the end of this chapter).

Dialog security has the advantage of encrypting and decrypting messages once, no matter how many Service Brokers the message is forwarded through on the way to its destination. If your network includes forwarding servers or you think it may in the future, setting up dialog security is probably worthwhile. The other advantage of dialog security is that you can configure different levels of security according to the security requirements of each service. For example, a service that returns catalogue information or inventory status may not require encryption, while a service that exchanges confidential customer information does.

If your network is secure enough so that encryption on the wire isn't required, or if transport security is sufficient, you may want to turn off dialog security. This is done by creating the dialog with the following command:

```
BEGIN DIALOG @ConversationHandle
      FROM SERVICE PrintResponse
      TO SERVICE 'PrintManuscript'
      WITH ENCRYPTION = OFF
```

Turning encryption off doesn't necessarily disable encryption for a dialog. **ENCRYPTION = OFF** means that encryption is not required. If the **TO SERVICE** has a **REMOTE SERVICE BINDING**, the dialog will be secured even when **ENCRYPTION = OFF** is used. If **ENCRYPTION = ON**, the **BEGIN DIALOG** statement will succeed but messages will be delayed if there is no **REMOTE SERVICE BINDING** or if dialog security isn't configured correctly. But when **ENCRYPTION = OFF**, the presence of a **REMOTE SERVICE BINDING** will determine if the dialog will be secured. This allows the application developer and the DBA to both have some influence on dialog security. The application developer may decide that certain dialogs should always be secured, so the **BEGIN DIALOG** statements are written to default to secure dialogs. Other dialogs may not always require security, so they will be started with the **ENCRYPTION = OFF** option. The DBA deploying the application must provide certificates for the dialogs that require security and can choose whether or not to configure security for the ones that don't.

The transport layer always signs messages and always requires authentication. Whether to use Windows or certificate-based authentication and whether to encrypt transport messages are options that the DBA can control. Because Windows authentication is simple to configure, it is the default authentication option. Certificate authentication is slightly harder to configure, but it works across domain boundaries without the complex trust configuration required for Windows authentication.

Whether to configure the transport connection to use encryption depends on the level of security required and whether dialog security is used. If the dialogs that carry confidential data are secured, it probably isn't necessary to encrypt the transport connection unless the highest level of security is required. Dialog security encrypts the message contents and leaves the routing information in clear text so that message forwarders can read it to route the message correctly. Message signing at the transport layer ensures that the headers are not altered, but if you want the messages headers to be encrypted or if there are some non-secure dialogs that use the connection, you may want to configure the connection to use encryption. Note that the transport encryption logic recognizes encrypted messages and doesn't double-encrypt secure dialogs, so the extra overhead of encrypting transport connections isn't that high for secure dialogs.

Summary of Permissions

Let's recap the permissions required for Service Broker dialogs:

▶ The user executing **BEGIN DIALOG, SEND, END CONVERSATION, MOVE DIALOG, RECEIVE,** or **GET CONVERSATION GROUP** commands must have **RECEIVE** permission on the queue associated with the **FROM SERVICE** of the dialog and **REFERENCES** permission on the contract used by the dialog.

▶ At the target side of the dialog, the user that owns the private key certificate representing the target service must have **CONTROL** permission on the target service.

▶ The user on the target side (the one who owns the public key corresponding to the private key owned by the user who owns the initiator service) must have **SEND** permission on the target service. If the dialog is anonymous, then **PUBLIC** must have **SEND** permission on the target service.

▶ The user specified in the **EXECUTE AS** clause of a queue with an activated stored procedure must have **RECEIVE** permission on the queue and **EXECUTE** permission on the stored procedure.

Replacing Certificates

We have discussed the procedure for replacing the certificates used for endpoint authentication by the transport connection. The certificates used for dialog authentication must also be replaced before they expire. This procedure also takes advantage of the ability of a single user to own multiple certificates.

The message transmission logic will choose a private key certificate owned by the owner of the **FROM SERVICE**. If this user owns more than one certificate, the certificate with the latest expiration date will be used. This can cause problems, because when a new private key certificate is created for the user, **BEGIN DIALOG** will immediately start using it because it will have the latest expiration date. These dialogs will fail until the public key for this certificate is exported and distributed to the target service. To get around this problem, the **ACTIVE FOR BEGIN_DIALOG** option for certificates will allow you to create a certificate but prevent its use in the **BEGIN DIALOG** command until the target endpoint is ready. Use the following command to create a new certificate that will not be used by the **BEGIN DIALOG** command:

```
CREATE CERTIFICATE PrinterResponseCertPriv2 AUTHORIZATION PrintResponseUser
       WITH SUBJECT = 'ForPrintResponse'
   ACTIVE FOR BEGIN_DIALOG =  OFF
```

Back up the public key portion of this certificate and import it as a certificate owned by the user that represents the initiator in the target database. When this is complete, dialogs will be able to use the new certificate. Use the following command to switch the **BEGIN DIALOG** statement to use the new certificate:

```
ALTER CERTIFICATE PrinterResponseCertPriv2
    WITH ACTIVE FOR BEGIN_DIALOG =  ON
```

Now that both the initiator and the target are using the new certificate, drop the old certificate from both the initiator and target databases. This won't affect existing dialogs because they have already exchanged a session key. They no longer need the certificates.

The certificate owned by the user that has **CONTROL** of the target service must also be replaced and the corresponding public key distributed to the initiators of the service. This should be done by first creating the private key certificate in the target database and then distributing the public key certificate to the initiators, where it will be owned by the user specified in the **REMOTE SERVICE BINDING** for the service.

Duplicate Services

Service Broker supports duplicate copies of the same service for load balancing or redundancy purposes. When Service Broker finds multiple routes to the same service, it randomly picks one of them to establish the new dialog. Service Broker distinguishes duplicate services at the routing level to route the messages to the correct instance, but in principle, each service with the same name offers exactly the same contract, including security requirements. Therefore, Service Broker expects all services of the same type to offer the same security.

There is only one **REMOTE SERVICE BINDING** for the service, so the same certificates will be used to authenticate to any of the duplicate services. Therefore, all the target service databases must use the same certificates. This means that the private key certificate must be propagated to all the duplicate databases. The **BACKUP CERTIFICATE** command supports dumping the private key to a file encrypted with a password and then creating a new certificate with the private key by specifying the password again. While this is a secure way to transfer a private key, it can be tedious if several certificates must be duplicated. In general, the easy way to produce duplicate services is to get one copy set up in a database and then use either **detach/attach** or **backup/restore** to duplicate the whole database with all the metadata and certificates.

Note:

Databases communicating within the same instance may need to be TRUSTWORTHY. A user in a database is considered to be equivalent to a user in another database in the same SQL Server instance if they both are associated with the same LOGIN. This means that when a user executes a command that crosses databases, the command will execute in the remote databases with the same user context as the equivalent user in the local database. This is acceptable when the user connects to the database through a normal login, but in SQL Server 2005, EXECUTE AS, BEGIN DIALOG and other new features allow a user to execute commands in the context of another user. This means that users can acquire privileges in another database in the instance without logging in to SQL Server as that user. Since this is a possible security threat, this cross-database impersonation is only allowed from trustworthy databases. If you want to begin an unsecured dialog with another database in the same instance, the database where the BEGIN DIALOG command is executed must be marked as trustworthy with the ALTER DATABASE <dbname> SET TRUSTWORTHY ON command. If you create the certificates and set up dialog security for the service, trustworthy is not required because the certificate establishes the user's identity in the target database.

Summary

Service Broker offers a wide variety of security features that allow you to build a secure, reliable messaging network with the correct amount of security for almost any network infrastructure. The unique security challenges of asynchronous messaging are satisfied by using the new certificate storage and encryption features of SQL Server 2005.

Advanced Topics

Chapter 12

Advantages of Service Broker

One of the most common questions I hear about Service Broker is "why do we need another messaging system?" I hope that after reading the book thus far you are convinced that Service Broker has a unique set of features that no other messaging system offers. In the remaining chapters, we will expand on this theme by describing why Service Broker exists and what kinds of applications you can build with it. This chapter discusses the unique features of Service Broker that make it possible to build a whole new class of reliable, asynchronous, distributed database applications. The next two chapters will discuss two key scenarios for Service Broker applications.

Loose Coupling

One of the most significant aspects of message-based applications is that they are loosely coupled. In a messaging application, *loose coupling* means that the services that make up the application only interact through messages. This is important because if two services understand the same set of messages, they can work together—even if they are implemented using different technologies, run on different platforms, exist in different locations, or even developed by different vendors. For example, if an order entry system communicates with the manufacturing system through a well-defined set of messages that both applications understand, the order entry system may be implemented as a .NET application running on Windows while the manufacturing system runs on a mainframe. Not only that, but multiple order entry systems implemented in different technologies on different platforms can all send orders to the same manufacturing system.

Service Broker has limited cross-platform abilities because it only works with services that use SQL Server 2005, but loose coupling is still a very valuable attribute of Service Broker applications because applications can be assembled from independent services that communicate with each other through well-defined messages. Because services only know about each other through the messages they exchange, a TSQL shipping service can communicate with a C++ inventory service or multiple inventory services written at different times running in different warehouses owned by different companies.

Loosely coupled services can be developed independently by different teams as long as the message formats don't change. Services that make up a loosely coupled Service Broker application can be rewritten, upgraded, and replaced independently as business needs change. One or two services can be changed to take advantage of new technology or changing business conditions without rewriting the whole application.

Reliable, asynchronous messaging makes loose coupling even more attractive. Wrapping a slow, outmoded system as part of a new application often limits the performance of the new application to the speed of the slowest component. For example, a new order entry system written with the latest technology can be brought to its knees by an ancient COBOL billing system that is just too expensive to replace. Wrapping the billing system as an asynchronous Service Broker service will allow the billing system to execute asynchronously at its own pace without slowing down the order entry system. Because Service Broker messages are queued reliably in the database, the application can send a billing message using Service Broker and be assured that it will be processed even if the billing system doesn't get around to it until well after the order is complete.

While it's not required for loose coupling, many loosely coupled systems use XML to define messages because XML can be processed by a wide variety of different technologies. For example, an application that used binary serialized .NET classes to define its messages would have difficulty communicating with a legacy C++ service. Service Broker can improve the reliability of XML messaging applications by enforcing standard XML schemas for messages. If a service needs to be able to accept messages from a variety of sources, Service Broker's schema validation for messages can simplify the service logic by ensuring that only messages that satisfy the message schema will be received by the service. Schema validation can be expensive from a processor utilization perspective, so it's probably not a good idea to use schema validation for every message. In general, validation is only justified when messages come from unknown or semi-trusted sources.

On the other hand, defining an XML schema for every message type is an excellent way to define the messaging interface between services, and using schema validation on every message during development and testing in an excellent way to catch errors early. The **ALTER MESSAGE TYPE** command makes it easy to enforce schema validation early in a project and then turn it off to improve performance once you're sure everything is working correctly.

As you can see, Service Broker supports loose coupling at the message data level and also loose coupling in time and space. Assembling applications from loosely coupled services tied together with reliable, asynchronous messaging provides a huge amount of flexibility in application development, configuration, and deployment.

Scalability

For the purposes of this chapter, I'll define *scaling* as adding processing resources to an application to increase the amount of load or the number of users it can handle. When a company deploys a new application, it needs to consider not only whether the application will be able to support the current processing load but whether it will be able to grow to support more processing load as the company grows or the application evolves. Application scalability is this ability to expand as needs expand.

There are two basic ways to scale an application. To *scale up* is to run the application on a bigger server. To *scale out* is to distribute the application across multiple servers. In general, it is much easier to scale up a database than to scale it out, because splitting data across multiple servers is difficult to get right and generally requires a significant amount of maintenance. On the other hand, there are many situations where scaling out an application is more cost-effective than scaling up. A Service Broker application can usually be scaled out effectively if it is designed for scalability. This section discusses how to design Service Broker applications for scalability.

There are two aspects to scaling out Service Broker applications. First, process intensive applications can scale out by adding more application processors to process messages from a queue. Second, database I/O-intensive applications can scale out by creating multiple copies of the database and distributing messages among the copies for processing.

Scaling Out Application Processors

The first scale out alternative is useful for services that primarily perform work outside the database. Figure 12.1 shows what a typical application deployment might look like.

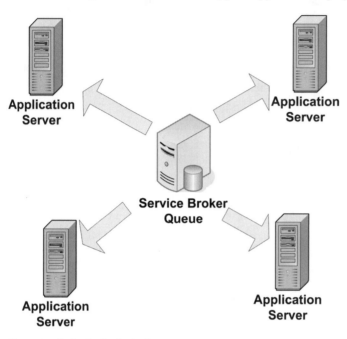

Figure 12.1: Scaling Out Application Processors.

Applications often include services that do most of their work outside the database. Typical examples are network operations such as Web service calls, disk file IO, e-mail, resource planning, and interest calculations. Currently, database applications that need to execute actions outside the database will use extended stored procedures or in SQL Server 2005, CLR stored procedures. While this is often a very effective way to do processor-intensive or non-database operations, the processing is done on database threads, so the database performance may be impacted. The Service Broker approach to this is to put the work to be processed on a Service Broker queue and then use one or more external applications to receive messages from the queue and process them. For example, if your application needs to make a Web services call to check a customer's credit history, you might put the customer's identification information on a Service Broker queue. An external application would receive these messages, send a SOAP message to the credit bureau and wait for the response. When the response is received, the application would send it as a Service Broker response message on the same dialog that the request was received on. The key point to understand in this service is that the majority of the time is spent waiting for the response from the credit service. If the credit service is a synchronous Web service, a thread is tied up waiting for the response. While CLR stored procedures make it possible to make the Web service call directly from the database, in that case the thread that's tied up waiting for the response is a database thread which then is not available to do other database work. Moving the Web services processing to another machine removes this overhead from the database threads and improves throughput.

Moving this processing off the database server to an application server also means it's very easy to scale out the processing when necessary. If the number of credit checks increases sharply (during Christmas season perhaps), additional application servers receiving requests from the same queue can be added with little effort. Nothing changes in the Service Broker configuration to enable this; you just deploy more copies of the same program. Service Broker conversation group locking ensures that related messages are processed together. The asynchronous nature of Service Broker applications means that when requests exceed the capacity of the available application processors, the queue just grows until the incoming rate goes down so the application processors can catch up, or until another application processor is added. Reliable queuing ensures that no requests are lost when demand exceeds the available resources. When the load returns to normal, the extra application servers can be removed and used for other purposes.

Scaling Out a Service Broker Service

While adding more processing power to processing messages from a single queue works well for processor-intensive or IO-intensive applications, database-intensive services require a different approach. I'm defining a *database-intensive service* as one that spends most of its time interacting with the database—either looking up data or updating the database. Trying to scale this kind of service by using multiple external application servers probably won't help much because the critical resource is the database itself. Often the best way to scale out this kind of service is to create multiple copies of the service on different database servers and distribute the request messages among the available services. Figure 12.2 illustrates a possible configuration.

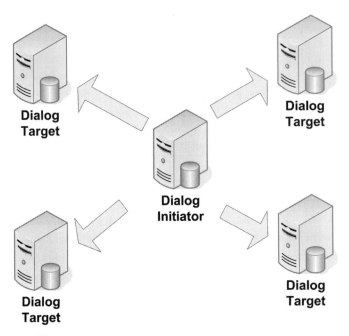

Figure 12.2: Scaling Out Service Broker Services.

When the dialog initiator needs to start a dialog with the target service, it picks one of the targets and begins the dialog to that target. In Chapter 10 we learned that if Service Broker finds multiple routes for the same service, it randomly picks one of the available routes to send the first message of the dialog to. After the first message, all subsequent messages on the same dialog must go to the same target instance of the service because that database is maintaining the endpoint state of the dialog.

Allowing the Service Broker routing logic to randomly pick a target from the list of available routes implies that all the targets are identical. This means that the target databases must be kept synchronized continuously, because it's hard to imagine an application that could tolerate getting a different answer depending on which target service was picked. The most common scenario for this type of scale out would be a service that looks up information from reasonably static data. One example may be parts lookup from a catalog that only changes a few hundred times a day. In this case, replication could easily keep the copies of the catalog synchronized with each other, so spreading the load among multiple identical copies of the catalog is a very practical option. Another example is a fairly small but heavily used data warehouse. One of the first Service Broker applications deployed used the dialogs to distribute queries to one of four identical data warehouses. This not only distributed the load but obviously provided fault tolerance. The data warehouse was updated at night. The daily updates were applied to all of the copies so they were always in sync. This was practical because the warehouse size was about 500 GB. Doing this with a 10 TB data warehouse obviously wouldn't be practical.

One thing to keep in mind when you are deploying multiple copies of the same service is that Service Broker assumes they are exactly the same service and any one it chooses will work exactly the same. This means, for example, that if this service includes certificates for dialog security, each copy must have exactly the same certificates. The easiest way to do this is to just copy the database, either by using database backup and restore or by using attach and detach and copying the database files. This way, all the certificates and keys will be copied. Remember that each copy is a new Service Broker instance, so you will have to specify **ENABLE_BROKER** and **NEW_BROKER** when you restore or attach the database. Also remember that the certificates are encrypted with the database master key, which is in turn encrypted with the service master key. Copying a database to another instance of SQL Server will change the service master key, so you will have to assign a password to the database master key with the **ALTER MASTER KEY** statement. This password will then be used when the database is copied to the new SQL Server instance to establish encryption for the certificates in the database with the new service master key.

In many cases, you may need to scale out a service when it is not practical to deploy multiple copies of the same service. An example might be the inventory for an online retailer. Each sale will make one or more changes to the inventory, so thousands of database updates a minute are probably not uncommon. Trying to keep multiple copies of this inventory synchronized with thousands of updates would not be practical in many cases. The overhead of applying each update to multiple copies of the database would cancel out most of the performance gains of scaling out the inventory service. In general, the best way to scale out a service that involves a high percentage of updates is to partition the database into multiple databases, each containing a well-defined subset of the data. Because a given item only exists in one of the databases, updating an item quantity only updates one database. This means that updates are spread across the databases instead of being duplicated in each database.

Not all database or all services can be partitioned effectively. Partitioning only makes sense when almost all services that use the database include the key that the database is partitioned on. To see what this means, let's use our inventory database as an example.

If the database is partitioned on item number ranges (0-10000 in one partition, 10001-20000 in the next, etc.), requests that include the item number can easily be directed to the correct database. On the other hand, requests that don't include the item number (requests that return a list of all items with a quantity less than 200) will have to execute in all the databases and the results from all the databases will have to be assembled and perhaps sorted. While SQL Server's distributed query feature can handle this kind of query, too many queries that span multiple databases will again cancel out many of the benefits of a partitioned database. For this reason, deciding whether partitioning makes sense and how best to partition a database requires careful analysis of the types of services required.

If you decide to partition your database, applications that use the partitioned service will have to be aware of the partitioning so that they can establish dialogs with the correct instance of the service. This means two things: 1) All the routes to the partitioned service must include the **BROKER_INSTANCE** parameter so you can direct dialogs to a particular instance; 2) All **BEGIN DIALOG** statements must specify the **service_ broker_guid** parameter of the correct database. The easiest way to do this is to wrap the **BEGIN DIALOG** statement in a function or procedure that looks up the correct database based on some data in the message—for example, based on the ISBN number of the book being ordered. The procedure might look up the **service_broker_guid** for the destination database, begin a conversation to that database, and then return the conversation handle.

Scaling Out a Service Broker Application

One of the advantages of the Service Broker style of loosely coupled asynchronous applications is that a correctly designed application can be scaled out by changing the Service Broker infrastructure without rewriting the application. An application made up of independent, loosely coupled services connected with asynchronous Service Broker messaging can run on a single server or on many servers equally well.

For example, Figure 12.3 shows a typical Service Broker order entry application with the application and four services running on a single server. The services communicate through service broker queues. Figure 12.4 shows the same application scaled out to five servers.

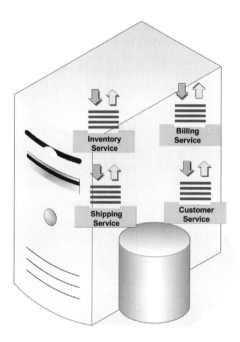

Figure 12.3: Order Entry Application.

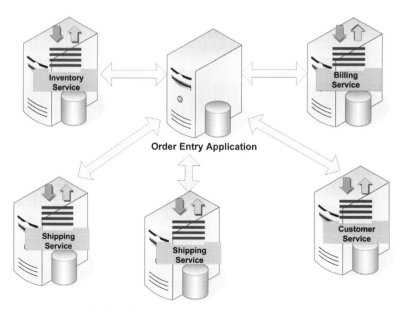

Figure 12.4: Scaled Out Order Entry Application.

The key thing to understand is that the difference between these two application deployments is the Service Broker routes used to route dialogs. The services themselves don't have to change. And the applications that call the services don't have to change.

Writing applications that can scale out easily requires that they be very loosely coupled. In the example above, if the shipping service looks up inventory locations in the inventory service's database, some of the performance advantage of moving them to separate servers is negated by the extra overhead of the shipping service doing distributed queries into the inventory database. If the shipping service requires a large amount of data from the inventory service, it may be necessary to replicate data to the shipping database when scaling out the database. If there are too many dependencies between services, it may not be possible to move them to separate servers when required. To avoid this issue, build the original application with each service in its own database, so that when you need to separate the services, it will be easy to move any service to another SQL Server instance by just moving the database.

The other thing worth noting in Figure 12.4 is that there are two types of scaling out illustrated. First, the application is scaled out by moving services to their own servers. Second, the shipping service is further scaled out by deploying two copies of the service. The shipping service may need enough resources so that two servers are required to handle the volume of requests. The more common reason for this type of scale out is that there are two different warehouses that ship orders, and each warehouse has its own shipping service. In this case, the shipping databases are probably partitioned so that each database only maintains data about its own shipments and the order entry application routes dialogs to the appropriate service based on where the order is to be shipped from.

This type of application scalability is especially interesting to software application developers because they can write a single application that can be deployed on a single server or scaled out to a number of different servers as required. A carefully designed application can be scaled for almost any size business by deploying it to the required number of servers.

Performance

Service Broker's support for asynchronous operations can significantly improve performance of many applications. The specific aspect of performance discussed in this section is the response time to the caller of an application function. The way Service Broker improves response time is by allowing parts of the function that can be safely deferred to execute after the response has been returned to the caller. For example, in the order entry application we discussed in the "Scalability" section, the order header and order lines must be written to the database before the order entry function completes—because the user may immediately check the status of the order. On the other hand, the other parts of the order—updating the inventory, billing, credit check, shipping, etc.—can safely be done after the original transaction commits. With Service Broker, the messages that will kick-off the background tasks are committed with the order header and order line inserts. This means that the application can rely on Service Broker to ensure that the background tasks are executed even though the original transaction is complete and control has been returned to the user before the background work has been done.

Parallel Stored Procedures

Another way that Service Broker can improve performance is by allowing services to be executed in parallel. SQL Server stored procedures are single threaded, so even though the queries executed by a stored procedure may use parallelism to execute, the stored procedure logic executes serially. Using Service Broker, it is possible for a stored procedure to asynchronously call multiple services that will then execute simultaneously. The original stored procedure can then wait for all the services to complete before returning.

A key concept to understand is that parallel execution of multiple services reduces the time that it takes to return a response to the user, but it does this at the cost of using more resources to produce the result. To understand this concept, think about a stored procedure that calls three other stored procedures. Normally, all four stored procedures— the original one and the three called by the original stored procedure—execute on a single SQL Server thread. Doing the same operation using Service Broker to make all the stored procedures execute in parallel returns the answer significantly sooner but uses four SQL Server threads to execute. This means that in general the number of simultaneous users that can call this stored procedure is reduced, even though the response time of the stored procedure is reduced. While in many cases this might be an acceptable tradeoff, parallel execution of a stored procedure is something that should only be used if response time is more important than resource usage. In reality, if many stored procedures calling services in parallel are executing simultaneously, some of the services will complete in less time than others and be available for calls from other procedures, so the total number of threads used will be less than you might expect. For example, a stored procedure that calls three services will use four threads when all the services are executing, but 50 of these stored procedures executing may only use 100 threads or less, instead of the 200 you might expect (because many of the services will share the same threads).

To see where parallel stored procedure execution is useful, consider the following call center application. When a customer calls, the application uses caller-id to find out who is calling and looks up all the information about that customer so that it can be displayed to the operator before the operator answers the call. The required information is located in five different applications, so five stored procedures are used to retrieve it. These stored procedures are very large and take an average of two seconds to execute. This means returning the information will take 10 seconds when the stored procedures are executed one after another. Ten seconds is a long time when you're waiting for help, so customer satisfaction scores would be low. If you rewrite this application so that the data-gathering stored procedures are implemented as Service Broker services and the main stored procedure calls all five stored procedures simultaneously, the operator can answer the call in an average of 2 seconds instead of 10. Running the application this way will consume more resources, but the improved customer satisfaction scores are probably worth it.

Listing 12.1 illustrates a stored procedure that calls three services simultaneously and waits for all three responses before returning.

```
CREATE PROCEDURE ParallelOrder as

DECLARE @message XML
SET @message =
N'<?xml version="1.0"?><ShippingRequest
➲  xmlns="http://schemas.adventure-works.com/demo/ShippingRequest"
➲  xmlns:xsi="http://www.w3.org/2001/XMLSchema-instance" >
        <SalesOrderID>87362</SalesOrderID>
        <Customer>
                <fname>Larry</fname>
                <lname>Simpson</lname>
                <address11>One Microsoft Way</address11>
```

```
              <city>Redmond</city>
              <state>WA</state>
              <country>USA</country>
      </Customer>
      <ProductDetail>
              <productID>83662</productID>
              <quantity>3</quantity>
              <price>3.14</price>
      </ProductDetail>
      <ProductDetail>
              <productID>263745</productID>
              <quantity>2</quantity>
              <price>19.95</price>
      </ProductDetail>
</ShippingRequest>';

DECLARE @OrderID uniqueidentifier
-- Create an Order id GUID and insert a recored into the state table
SET @OrderID = NEWID()
Insert into OEState values (@OrderID, N'Initial', 0, 0, 0)

BEGIN TRANSACTION;

-- Start the three dialogs
DECLARE @PODialog uniqueidentifier
BEGIN DIALOG @PODialog FROM SERVICE [OrderEntryService]
        TO SERVICE 'SOAPOService'  ON CONTRACT POContract
        WITH RELATED_CONVERSATION_GROUP = @OrderID;

DECLARE @InventoryDialog uniqueidentifier
BEGIN DIALOG @InventoryDialog FROM SERVICE [OrderEntryService]
        TO SERVICE 'SOAInventoryService'  ON CONTRACT InventoryContract
        WITH RELATED_CONVERSATION_GROUP = @OrderID;

DECLARE @CreditDialog uniqueidentifier
BEGIN DIALOG @CreditDialog FROM SERVICE [OrderEntryService]
```

```
        TO SERVICE 'SOACreditCheckService' ON CONTRACT CreditContract
        WITH RELATED_CONVERSATION_GROUP = @OrderID;

-- SEND the message to the services in parallel

SEND ON CONVERSATION @CreditDialog MESSAGE TYPE [OrderMessage](@message);
SEND ON CONVERSATION @PODialog MESSAGE TYPE [OrderMessage](@message);
SEND ON CONVERSATION @InventoryDialog MESSAGE TYPE [OrderMessage] (@message);

-- Update the state table to indicate that the messages have been sent
Update OEState SET Status = N'Messages Sent' WHERE OrderID = @OrderID

-- Commit the transaction - the transaction must be commmitted so the
--  message will be sent
COMMIT

--------------------------------------------------------------------

-- Wait for responses
-------------------------------------------------------------------------
DECLARE @conversationHandle uniqueidentifier
declare @message_body nvarchar(MAX)
declare @message_type_name sysname;

-- Normal Service Broker Receive loop
WHILE 1 = 1
begin
        BEGIN TRANSACTION
        WaitFor (
        RECEIVE top(1)
                @message_type_name=message_type_name,
                @conversationHandle=conversation_handle,
                @message_body=message_body
                FROM OrderQueue
                WHERE  conversation_group_id = @OrderID
        ), Timeout 6000
```

```
IF @@rowcount = 0
BEGIN
        ROLLBACK
        BREAK
END
-- When response message is received update the state
-- table to indicate that the service is complete
IF @message_type_name = N'CreditStatus'
        BEGIN
                -- message processing goes here
                UPDATE OEState SET CRDone = 1
                    WHERE OrderID = @OrderID
                END CONVERSATION @conversationHandle
        END
IF @message_type_name = N'InventoryStatus'
        BEGIN
                -- message processing goes here
                UPDATE OEState SET INVDone = 1
                    WHERE OrderID = @OrderID
                END CONVERSATION @conversationHandle
        END
IF @message_type_name = N'POInformation'
        BEGIN
                -- message processing goes here
                UPDATE OEState SET PODone = 1
                    WHERE OrderID = @OrderID
                END CONVERSATION @conversationHandle
        END

UPDATE OEState SET Status = N'Messages Received'
          WHERE OrderID = @OrderID and INVDone = 1 and
          PODone = 1 and CRDone = 1
```

```
        IF @@rowcount = 1
        BEGIN
                COMMIT
                BREAK
        END
        ELSE
                COMMIT


END
```

Listing 12.1: Parallel Stored Procedure Processing.

The procedure in Listing 12.1 starts by beginning three dialogs to the three different services required. Since the order number in this sample is a **uniqueidentifier** datatype, we can use it as the **conversation_group_id** in the **BEGIN DIALOG** command. The order number is also used as the primary key in the **OEState** table that we use to store the state of the conversation. After the three dialogs are started, a message is sent on each one to start the three services. The message body for all three messages is the same, to reduce the size of the example. After the messages are sent, the initial transaction is committed. This is very important because the messages aren't exposed on the target queue until the transaction that does the sends commits. This also means that this stored procedure can execute inside another transaction because the send transaction won't complete.

After the sends are complete, the stored procedure goes into a standard receive loop to wait for the responses. Notice that the **RECEIVE** statement specifies the **conversation_ group_id** in the WHERE clause so that it will only receive messages for this order. In a real application, there would be some processing for the returned messages to handle errors, update the order status, etc. For this example, the state entry in the **OEState** table entry for this order is updated to indicate that the response has been received. The last part of response handling checks to see if all the responses have been received and breaks out of the loop when all the status columns are set to 1, which indicates that all the response messages have been received and processed. At this point, you may be wondering why I chose to keep the status of the messages received in a table instead of just using variables to track which messages have been received. This is done to ensure that the state won't be lost if the system goes down for some reason. Service Broker messages survive system outages so the message handling must also be reliable. To keep thing simple, I haven't written the restart logic for this procedure, but after a system restart, the state of all orders would be checked and the order would either continue or be deleted depending on what the business logic requires.

As you can see, asynchronous processing can improve the performance of database applications by providing control over when the services that the application uses are processed. This doesn't reduce the total amount of processing that has to be done—in reality it generally increases the total amount of processing—but it reduces the length of time the user has to wait.

Transactional Messaging

In all the examples in this book, Service Broker commands are executed in the context of a transaction. In fact, because Service Broker is built into the database, anything it does that involves updating the database should be done within a transaction. This includes starting dialogs, sending and receiving messages, and even all the background processing like putting messages received from the network into queues, updating the **sys.conversation_ endpoints** tables when messages are sent or received, and updating status in the **sys. transmision_queue**. Transactions ensure that the messages in the queue stay consistent in spite of any errors or system failures. This transactional consistency is one of the most valuable aspects of Service Broker messaging.

Most messaging systems support *transactional messaging*. For our purposes, I'll define transactional messaging as a messaging system where sending or receiving a message can be placed in a transaction, so that the **SEND** operation doesn't put the message on a queue until the transaction commits, and the **RECEIVE** operation doesn't remove the message from the queue unless the transaction commits. The primary difference between Service Broker and many other messaging systems is that other messaging systems have transaction logic added to the message store and transactional messaging is one of several options. With Service Broker, transactional messaging is the only thing we do, and Service Broker is built into the mature, high-performance transaction system of SQL Server.

Transactional messaging means you can put message receives, message sends, updates to state tables, and updates to application data into a single transaction. A typical Service Broker transaction includes the following steps:

1. Receive one or more messages from the input queue.

2. Retrieve the state information associated with the conversation group of the message.

3. Process the message and make the appropriate updates to application data in the database.

4. Send one or more messages. These can be either responses to a message or requests to other services.

5. Update the state with the results of processing these messages.

Because this is all done in the same transaction, if any of these steps fails, the whole transaction rolls back and all the work is undone. For example, if there is a failure while updating the application state, the response message doesn't get sent, the state returns to its original values, and the received messages are put back on the queue. Everything is back to the way it was before the message was received and the messages are on the queue, ready to be processed again. This kind of error handling makes applications easy to write and debug.

Transactional messaging is also the only way to ensure "exactly once" message processing. Without transactions, there are always situations that would cause a message to be skipped or processed twice. For example, if a system loses power after a message was processed, but before it has been removed from the queue, the message will be processed again when the system comes up after power is restored. If you delete the message from the queue before processing it to avoid this problem, there's a chance that the message will be deleted without being processed so the message is lost. Making the message deletion and message processing part of the same transaction ensures that either the message will be processed and deleted or not processed and not deleted. Although there are techniques using sequence numbers and message status bits to get around these problems, these techniques amount to implementing transactional messaging without transactions. All the extra coding to make this work is avoided with transactional messaging.

Messaging in the Database

I hope by now you have a good understanding of why Service Broker is built into the database. In this section, we'll discuss a few more advantages of messaging in the database. We have already seen the advantages of transactional messaging for developing reliable asynchronous applications. With messaging built into the database, a single transaction can cover both the messaging operations and the database updates. When the message store is outside the database, transactional messaging requires two phase commits between the database and message store for every transaction. Handling both the messaging and database updates in a single database transaction is more reliable and yields better performance.

Having queues in the database means that all the database features that ensure data integrity for database data—transaction logs, clusters, database mirroring, etc.—apply equally to the messages. This is a very important part of asynchronous application design, because in this type of application, messages are valuable business objects. If the message from the order entry application to the shipping service gets lost, the order won't be shipped, and this leads to customer dissatisfaction. In a Service Broker application, the message won't be lost unless the database data is also lost. Therefore, you can be sure that the messages in the queues have the same degree of reliability and data integrity as the data associated with the service. Database backup and restore will work on both the data and the messages. Also, because they are both in the same backup file, the data and messages are always restored to the same point in time. With an external message store, it's easy for the messages and data to get out of sync when one or the other is restored from backup.

Another advantage of messaging in the database is that the tools used to program and manage the database data apply equally well to message queues. For example, if you want to know what messages are waiting to be processed, you don't have to write messaging code to look at the queue. Instead, you just write a **SELECT** statement against the view for the queue. If you want to know whether a message has been sent yet, you can query the **sys.transmission_queue** to see whether it's there or not. Developers who are using ADO. NET to write their database applications can use the tools they're familiar with to write the messaging part of the application.

When is Service Broker the Right Answer?

Now that we've discussed the advantages of Service Broker, we can answer the question of what kinds of applications work best with Service Broker and what kinds of applications should use other messaging alternatives. This question is usually asked like this: "There are already so many messaging products out there, why are you building yet another one?" I hope that this book has demonstrated to you some of the unique capabilities of Service Broker and that you enthusiastically agree that Service Broker is not just another messaging product. Service Broker fills a void that no other messaging product fills. In this section, I'll define what that void is and where Service Broker fits and doesn't fit.

As I have said several times in this book, Service Broker is a platform for building reliable, asynchronous, database applications. If your application doesn't fit that description, Service Broker may not be a good fit. First, if your application isn't a database application, Service Broker may not be a good fit. On the other hand, most applications store data or state somewhere, so if you're looking to improve the reliability of a messaging application, it may make sense to add SQL Server to the application to improve messaging reliability and improve the data integrity of the other data that your application maintains.

Even if your application uses a database, Service Broker might not be a good answer if the services you communicate with are not database applications. This is especially true if the remote service runs on a platform that doesn't support SQL Server. Incorporating SQL Server and Service Broker into the remote services your application communicates with will improve the reliability and data integrity of messaging. If that is an issue, Service Broker may be the right answer. On the other hand, adding a SQL Server database to the remote service will most likely require more maintenance than the same service without a database. This extra maintenance effort may be justified by the increase in reliability and recoverability that SQL Server offers.

Other messaging systems offer a range of services, from "best effort" to transactional messaging. Service Broker offers only transactional messaging, so if your application doesn't require the reliability of Service Broker, something like MSMQ or Notification Services might be a better choice. For example, if your application is sending stock prices or weather conditions as messages, it really doesn't matter if a few messages get lost here and there because another one will come along shortly. Losing a message only delays the information a little. In this situation, the highly reliable messaging of Service Broker is probably unnecessary.

Another limitation of the current Service Broker implementation is that Service Broker runs in a SQL Server instance. This means that if your application must communicate cross-platform, Service Broker won't work. Web Services are a better cross-platform answer. Most Web Services also communicate over HTTP networks, so they are a better answer in situations where security standards don't permit TCP/IP connection except through HTTP. The Service Broker team recognizes that the lack of support for Web Services protocols limits the networking options for Service Broker. They are looking seriously at offering Service Broker communications over Web Service protocols in a future release.

I get quite a few questions about the relationship between Service Broker and BizTalk. After all, both products move messages between queues in SQL Server databases. The choice between BizTalk and Service Broker depends on what your application needs to do besides moving messages between queues. BizTalk offers a wide variety of capabilities that Service Broker doesn't offer, such as message transformation, orchestrating message processing, and communicating with a wide variety of applications and messaging protocols. If your application needs these capabilities then it should use BizTalk. However, if you need efficient transfer of messages between SQL Server queues, Service Broker will do this more efficiently, precisely because it doesn't include all the advanced capabilities that BizTalk offers.

I want to emphasize that Service Broker isn't the answer for all messaging requirements, but if your application fits into Service Broker's capabilities, it offers unprecedented levels of reliability and performance for distributed, asynchronous database applications. The other thing to remember is that Service Broker offers significant advantages for building database applications even if the whole application uses only a single database. The asynchronous, queued capabilities of Service Broker coupled with Service Broker activation can be used to build scalable, asynchronous database applications even if there's no requirement for distribution.

Summary

In this chapter we stepped back from the details of building Service Broker applications to discuss the advantages that Service Broker provides for application developers. Loose coupling, scalability, performance, transactional messaging, and database messaging support allows the building of a whole new class of reliable, asynchronous database applications that were difficult or impossible to build before.

Did you know?

A BEGIN DIALOG command without an ENCRYPTION = NO clause requires a database master key. While a master key won't always be required, using the CREATE MASTER KEY command to create one in any database that has Service Broker queues is a good idea. Remember to put the password somewhere safe, because you will need it if you move the database. See Chapter 11 for more information.

Chapter 13

Reliable Service-Oriented Architecture

I hesitate to use the term "Service-Oriented Architecture" because it has been abused badly, but it actually describes Service Broker applications reasonably well. An application built with a Service-Oriented Architecture consists of loosely coupled, reusable services tied together with messages. The services are loosely coupled because the messages define the interface to the service. All internal details of the service not exposed through messages are hidden. As we saw in Chapter 12, this is a good description of a Service Broker application—independent services linked together with messages.

While most discussions of Service-Oriented Architectures involve Web services standards, the architecture doesn't require standardized messaging. Web services-based messaging offers the advantages of interoperability among a number of platforms, but if your application doesn't require interoperability, non-standards-based messaging works equally well. This chapter shows how the unique features of Service Broker make it an ideal platform for reliable service-oriented applications. We'll also discuss how to build reliable service-oriented applications with Service Broker and how to turn existing applications into Service Broker applications.

Reliable Messaging

Reliable, transactional messaging makes service-oriented applications much easier to implement. Without reliable, transactional messaging, the application must be prepared to deal with message delivery issues. For example, if a banking application sends a message to a checking account service asking for it to transfer money, what does the banking application do if it doesn't receive a response to the message? If it sends the message again after a certain time, there is a possibility that the original transfer succeeded but the response was lost—so now the transfer will happen twice. The only safe thing to do in that case is for the banking application to ask the checking service if it has processed the transfer and then resubmit the transfer request if it hasn't. Of course, if the checking service is down for some reason, the query for the transfer status will fail, so the banking system will have to continue to retry the request until the checking service comes back up. While this works, it adds a great deal of complexity to the application. Contrast this complexity with the Service Broker approach which is to do a reliable, transactional send and then be assured that either the transfer will be processed exactly once, or an error will be reliably returned to the banking application.

Asynchronous messaging also adds value to service-oriented applications. In the banking example, the banking application can send the transfer request message to the checking service and then go on to handle other tasks without waiting around for the response from the checking service. This makes applications more efficient but it also introduces some added complexity, because when the response does come back from the checking service, the banking application has moved on. To handle this issue, the banking service must maintain state about the service requests it has pending so that when the responses come back, the banking application remembers what to do with them. Fortunately, as we learned in Chapter 7, Service Broker makes handling state pretty simple.

Fault-Tolerant SOA

There are many reliable messaging infrastructures that can be used to implement service-oriented applications, but because Service Broker is built into SQL Server, the fault-tolerant features of SQL Server can be used to build fault-tolerant applications that offer extremely high availability.

Service Broker applications store the data a service uses, the state of service requests, and the incoming and outgoing messages in the same database. This means that for a properly designed service, the database contains everything the service needs to continue running, so all we have to do to protect the service from failures is to preserve the database. There are several ways to implement a fault-tolerant SQL Server database, including Windows clustering and log-shipping. However, this chapter emphasizes using Database Mirroring for fault tolerance, because the tight link between Service Broker and Database Mirroring offers some unique advantages for fault-tolerant services.

As discussed in Chapter 10, when a Service Broker application opens a connection to a mirrored pair of databases, it connects to both the primary and the secondary databases.

When Service Broker is running in a database that is a Database Mirrored database, it listens for the event that Database Mirroring sends when the secondary database becomes the primary. Service Broker sends a message to all brokers that have connections open to the database, informing them that the secondary database has now become the primary. This means that the remote broker can immediately start sending messages to the new primary. Failover happens in a few seconds instead of the minute or more that most other fault-tolerant solutions require for the connections to timeout and get re-established to the new primary. Figure 13.1 illustrates a Service Broker dialog before and after failover of a database mirror.

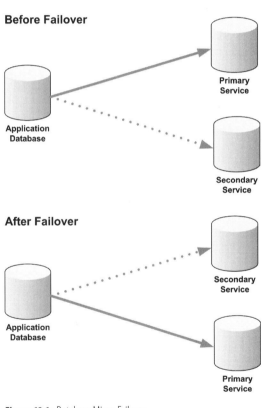

Figure 13.1: Database Mirror Failover.

The key to maintaining application consistency during the failover is transactional messaging. With transactional messaging, when a service fails over, any transactions in progress roll back, and because any messages were received as part of the transaction, they will still be on the queue on the new primary database. Therefore, they will be processed again with no loss of data. Because any changes to the state and the database were done as part of the same transaction, the messages can be processed again without fear of duplicating data.

Another advantage of Database Mirroring in service-oriented applications is that mirroring happens at the database level. This means that a SQL Server instance can have some databases that are primary databases and others that are secondary. This can allow better resource usage than a typical warm-standby configuration, because databases spread across two SQL Server instances can be consolidated into a single instance when a failure occurs. Figure 13.2 shows how this might work.

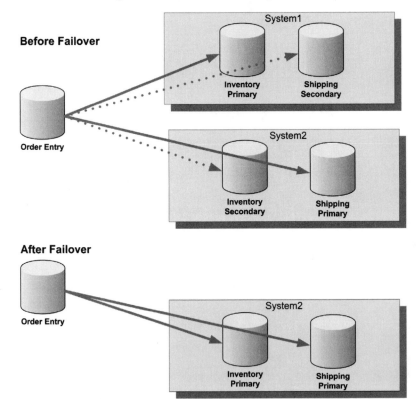

Figure 13.2: Multiple Database Failover.

As you can see, the Inventory service has failed over to System2 and the Shipping service continues to run on System2. The advantage of using Database Mirroring in this way is that both before and after failover, there are two databases running on each instance. This means that you don't have unused resources reserved on each server, waiting for the other server to fail. All the available memory can be allocated to each instance in this configuration. If you used these same two instances with Windows clustering, each server would have to leave enough memory unused to accommodate the other instance when it failed over. This configuration may require more disk space because there are two copies of each database, but the disk subsystem doesn't have to be as fault-tolerant (and expensive) as in a Windows cluster. The downside of database mirroring is that the mirroring process may require more network and disk bandwidth than Windows clustering.

A Service Broker application also allows for fault tolerance for the service processing code. If the service is implemented as a stored procedure, then the service code fails over when the database fails over. If the service processing code is an external application, then having all the data, messages, and state in the database means that the external processes can come and go without affecting the persistent state of the service. For example, if your application has two servers processing messages from the same queue, either one of them could fail without causing a problem. Any transactions in process would be rolled back and the remaining server would continue uninterrupted. External processes that are processing messages on mirrored databases should be listening for Database Mirroring state change events, so that they know when the database primary has changed. They can switch their database connections to the new primary database immediately.

Reliable Clients

We have seen how reliable transactional messaging and SQL Server fault tolerance make Service Broker a great platform for service-oriented applications, but we haven't discussed how clients connect to these applications. If clients connect through Web browsers of unreliable Web service interfaces, there is a layer of unreliable communications on top of the reliable application. If your application must service millions of clients or if the clients are only occasional users of your application, then unreliable clients are probably your only option. You have to deal with the issues of lost and duplicate messages at the client interface layer. On the other hand, if the clients of your application are heavy users of your application and are running on systems you have some influence over, it may make sense to extend reliability all the way to the client by using Service Broker dialogs for client communication also.

Using Service Broker for client communications is especially attractive if your application needs a database at the client anyway. For example, a point of sale terminal needs a place to store items and prices and a place to hold sales transactions for transfer to the back-end server. A SQL Express database running in the POS terminal would fulfill these requirements and also provide reliable communications through Service Broker. If the network or the host application isn't available, the POS terminal can continue to operate by queuing the sales transactions as Service Broker messages, which will be sent when the connection to the application is restored. Service Broker also has the advantage of being bi-directional: the application can push data (like new items or price changes) out to the POS terminals without the need for the POS terminal to ask for them. There are very few client connection technologies that allow the server to push unsolicited data to the client reliably.

There are many other applications that can benefit from reliable, bi-directional communications with the client. Shop floor applications need to be able to run even when the back-end systems are not available, so Service Broker can be used to queue messages for transmission when the connection is restored. Service Broker can also deal with bursts of data that are generated faster than the network can handle them by queuing them temporarily until the network catches up.

The disadvantage of using Service Broker for client communications is that you must install, configure, and maintain a database at every client. Again, if the client needs a database anyway, this is no problem. But if you are using Service Broker on the client purely for reliable communications, you have to balance the advantages of reliable communications against the extra maintenance overhead of a database on every client. With more emphasis on smart client applications, significant client applications without a local database will become rare over time. Therefore, having a database available for reliable communications will not be hard to achieve. In many cases, the advantages of reliable bi-directional communications with a client will outweigh the extra maintenance required to support a database on every client.

Building Reliable Service-Oriented Applications

Now that you're convinced that you should use Service Broker as the infrastructure for service-oriented applications, we will spend the rest of this chapter discussing how to design and build Service Broker applications. We have already covered the low-level details of how Service Broker applications work, so this section will cover the high-level architectural concepts required for service-oriented application development using Service Broker.

We will cover two kinds of application development—updating an existing application to use Service Broker and designing a new Service Broker application. Because many of the concepts are the same, I won't cover the two approaches separately, but I will call out the differences in approach as they come up.

Choosing an Application

One of the keys to success in service-oriented application development is choosing an application that is well suited to being implemented as a set of loosely coupled services. While most significant server applications can benefit from asynchronous services, breaking the wrong application into services may actually decrease performance and scalability. While there is no substitute for careful analysis, here are some rules of thumb that will help identify applications that are good candidates for Service Broker implementation:

▶ **Large, complex applications** — Applications with many components and procedures are very likely to have routines that can easily be isolated into loosely coupled services. This will not only improve the performance and reliability of the application, but the services can be reused in other applications. While large, complex applications often benefit more than smaller applications from service orientation, I usually recommend starting with a smaller application to learn how it's done and understand the benefits of service orientation before taking on a huge project.

▶ **Performance issues** — Chapter 12 showed how moving the less time-critical parts of your application to asynchronous services can improve the performance and responsiveness of the central, synchronous part of the application. Look at an application that is experiencing performance problems to find reasonably independent pieces of logic that can be executed after the main transaction has committed without violating the business constraints of the application. Also, loosely coupled services can be executed in parallel, which can improve performance even if all the services must complete before control is returned to the caller. Careful analysis of the control flow of the application and the business requirements is required to determine which services can be executed after control is returned to the caller, and which services must be completed before returning control. Both types of asynchronous services will improve performance and most applications will use a combination of the two types of services.

► **High reliability requirements** — When applications have extremely high availability requirements, the data integrity, reliability, and fault tolerance provided by the combination of Service Broker and the fault-tolerant features of SQL Server offer a unique platform for building highly reliable applications. Because all the persistent elements of a Service Broker application are stored in the database, the integrity of the application is assured as long as the database is preserved. Transactions which span data, state, and messages preserve the application's integrity in spite of failures. Fault-tolerant features such as database mirroring provide rapid recovery.

► **Need for scale out** — While scaling up databases is often the best choice because it doesn't require distribution or partitioning of data, there are some instances where scaling out applications is practical and more economical than scaling up. The easiest type of application to scale out using Service Broker is one where the database doesn't need to scale out, but the processing power needs to be expanded. Typical examples would be extremely processor-intensive applications like financial modeling or simulations. In this type of application, many processor nodes can connect to a single database queue and receive messages containing the work to be done. They can process the work contained in the message and return results or status to a results queue in the database. This can also be a very fault-tolerant solution. If one of the worker processors crashes, the messages it was processing will reappear on the queue when the transaction rolls back and another processor can pick up the work. Using many processors to process work from a single queue works well when the jobs to be processed require a lot of processing time or are waiting for disk or network I/O. Work items that are highly parallel can also benefit from having many parallel process executions that receive work from a single queue. Chapter 14 covers using Service Broker to schedule work.

▶ **Need for distribution** — Many enterprises have operations in widely
separated geographic locations. In many cases, it will be more efficient
to distribute an application across these locations. For example, placing
shipping services in the shipping warehouses or manufacturing services
in widely dispersed plants will not only lead to more efficient and timely
processing but also make these operations less susceptible to network
failures. If you decide to distribute services closer to where they are used to
improve network fault tolerance, reliable messaging will allow the services
to operate independently when the network is unavailable and catch up
automatically when connectivity is restored. Storing messages in database
queues ensures that they won't be lost in case of network or power failures.

While there are many other types of applications that can benefit from reliable, fault-
tolerant services, these five types should be enough to get you thinking about whether the
Service Broker style of application will work for you. You must carefully analyze your
requirements to determine whether Service Broker is a good solution to you application
issues is the same—whether you are modifying an existing application or designing a new
one. The key to designing this type of application is identifying the parts of the application
that can become services, which can be processed at another time, another place, or in
parallel. The next section describes how to identify those services.

Choosing Services

Choosing services that can be run asynchronously (and possibly remotely) is a key factor
in designing a service-oriented application. These are the characteristics you should look
for when designing a service or choosing part of an existing application to convert into a
service:

▶ **Asynchronous or parallel execution possible** — Much of the value of
using services derives from their being asynchronous and loosely coupled.
If you choose services which don't fit this description, you may not see
much benefit from a service-oriented architecture. Whether a function
or procedure is suitable for an asynchronous service is often more a
business question than a technical question. For example, do the rules of
your business allow you to take an order for an item based on Available To
Promise estimates, or do they require that specific items in inventory be

allocated to the order before it is complete? If the former is true, inventory allocation can be an asynchronous service, while if the latter is true, inventory allocation must be done synchronously.

Look for parts of the process which can reasonably be executed at a later time or in another place without violating the basic business rules that the application must obey. Also remember that synchronous activities may make good services if they can be executed in parallel. Starting a number of services in parallel and then waiting for all the results before proceeding— as in the parallel stored procedure example in Chapter 12—can improve performance without violating business rules that require the services to be complete before the process finishes.

As an example of choosing services, see the order entry process diagram in Figure 13.3.

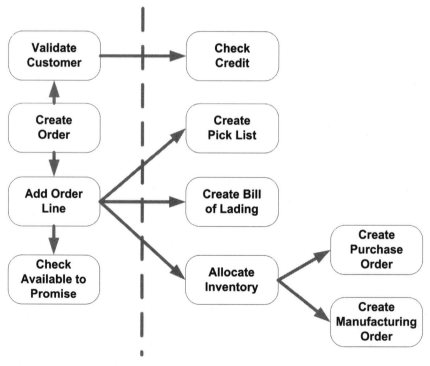

Figure 13.3: Order Entry Process.

In the figure, the items to the left of the dotted line must all be completed before the order is committed to the database. The order header and order lines are necessary because the user may inquire about their order immediately after entering it. The customer must pass the initial validation process so that orders are not accepted from bogus customers, and the items in the order must be available in the requested time frame.

The parts of the process to the right of the dotted line in Figure 13.3 can all be executed asynchronously because the business rules of our hypothetical organization allow them to happen after the initial order has been committed to the database. In general, as these services complete, the status of the order will change (from credit pending to credit approved, for example). A customer checking on the order will see the status change over time as the asynchronous services complete. In some cases, it may take weeks or months for all the asynchronous services to complete. If you ordered a commercial jetliner for example, the Manufacturing process takes some time.

The process of breaking an application into individual processes and determining which of them would make good services is the basis of successful service-oriented design.

▶ **Undoable or cancellable** — The most radical change required when converting a function to an asynchronous service is making it undoable. Because each service executes in its own transaction, you can't rely on transaction rollback to clean up after a failure or error. For example, in the order entry process in Figure 13.3, if the inventory allocation fails—perhaps because the item is no longer made—all the other parts of the order must be undone, even if they are already committed to the database. While undoing a committed transaction is a radical concept to most database developers, in reality, many business processes are already cancellable. For example, cancelling an order because the customer changed her mind or cancelling a shipment because the order was cancelled are common actions. If the order and shipment must be cancelled because the inventory allocation failed, it shouldn't require radical changes to the application. However, if you can't come up with a reasonable way to cancel or undo the effects of a service, it probably should be done as part of the initial transaction, so that it can be rolled back if necessary.

▶ **Not too tightly coupled** — Services that are tightly coupled to the rest of the application generally can't be used as effectively in scale-out scenarios or reused in other applications. For example, if the shipping service obtains most of the data it needs from the inventory database, it will be hard to scale out the application by running these two services on different servers. If the credit check part of the application accesses a significant amount of global data from the customer and order functions, it may be impossible to isolate it as an asynchronous service without a significant amount of rewriting. While this effort might be justified if the potential for performance improvement or reuse of the service is large, a very tightly coupled function usually doesn't make a good asynchronous service.

On the other hand, a tightly coupled function—like the shipping service that relies on the inventory database—may still make a good service if asynchronous execution provides enough payback by itself. Even if the two services can never be physically located in different databases, having them execute in parallel may improve performance enough to justify the effort to make them into services. You may also decide that the shipping service would be usable in a number of other applications, which might justify the effort of converting it to a service.

While it's difficult to make definitive statements about which parts of an application should or shouldn't be built as services, I think any part of the application that meets these three criteria should be strongly considered for implementation as a service.

Defining Messages and Dialogs

Once you have chosen a suitable application to implement or re-implement as a service-oriented application and determined which services you need to create, the next step is to define the Service Broker messages and dialogs that will connect the services together. While this part of the design is very dependant on the application, this section discusses some things you should consider while designing the messages and dialogs.

Loose Coupling vs. Message Size

We have already discussed the advantages of loosely coupled services, but loose coupling often comes at the expense of larger messages. For example, a message to a loosely coupled shipping service would include all the information required to ship the items—customer information, order information, order lines, commitment dates, etc. This allows the shipping service to run in a separate database in a remote location without depending on data in the order database. On the other hand, a message to the shipping service that includes just the order number of the order to ship means that the shipping service is tightly coupled to the order database. It will have to look into the order database for the information it needs, but as long as the shipping service runs on the same server as the order service, this may be the most efficient way to implement the service, especially if you are reusing code that already works this way.

Sending all the information required to a loosely coupled service makes your application much more flexible and scalable. It improves reusability of the services, but this must be weighed against the extra size of messages in the Service Broker queues and the overhead of serializing the information into the message and deserializing it in the service. In general, you should look at the short term and long term probability of moving the service to another database when deciding how loosely coupled your service should be. Moving many megabytes of messages between services running in the same database may turn out to be a high price to pay for the flexibility of moving the service to another database at some later time. I encourage you to use the loosely coupled approach if possible, but practical considerations might caution against this.

XML or Binary

One of the more common questions I hear is whether Service Broker messages should be XML or binary. It depends. Using XML as the message body provides a lot of options for implementing the service. Any language or platform that can parse XML can process an XML message, so XML message bodies will allow you to change implementations without changing the messages. This is one of the primary advantages of service-oriented applications. On the other hand, sending binary data as XML can be inefficient and involve significant processing overhead. Fortunately, Service Broker handles both XML and binary data as message bodies.

The ordering of dialog messages makes it easier to handle a mixture of XML and binary data. For example, if your service accepts employee data which includes a textual data and a photograph, the service can accept an XML message with the textual data followed by a binary message with the photograph. Because the dialog ensures that the XML message will be processed first and the binary message will be processed next, the service can rely on getting both messages in a predictable order. There's no need for the complexity of encoding the picture as XML data so that it can be sent in a single message.

If you decide to use XML data as the message body, the message design should include an XML schema to document the format of the messages. This not only makes it easier to write the services, but the schema validation features of Service Broker message types can be used to ensure that only messages that follow the schema will be delivered. Schema validation can be fairly expensive if the messages are large and complex. Therefore, you might want to use schema validation during development and testing and then use **ALTER MESSAGE TYPE** to turn off validation in production.

The key point here is that Service Broker is equally effective at handling XML and binary messages. Your decision should be based on the type of data you need to transfer and how much platform independence you want to build into your application.

Dialog Patterns

One of the common misconceptions about Service Broker dialogs is that they only support request-response messaging. I'll plead guilty to fostering this misconception by writing most of the samples this way. Request-response (a message from the initiator to the target, followed by a message from the target back to the initiator) is the most common messaging pattern. It's the way remote procedure calls and Web requests work. While Service Broker does an excellent job of supporting the request-response messaging pattern, Service Broker's persistent dialogs offer many more interesting messaging patterns that many messaging systems don't support.

One of the more interesting messaging patterns supported by Service Broker is the reliable stream of ordered messages. In this pattern, a stream of messages is sent from one endpoint to the other with little or no response traffic in the opposite direction. Service Broker ensures that these messages will be delivered and processed in order. There's really no need for a response unless there is something wrong with one of the messages. A good example of this pattern would be the Point of Sale terminal. The POS terminal would send a continuous stream of customer transactions to the store computer or to the home office. The home office would send a stream of price changes and new item records back to the POS terminal. Neither of these streams requires a response for every message sent. If the network goes down, the streams build up at both endpoints. When the connection is restored, the streams catch up. Because there is no response to each message, the reliable stream is a very efficient way to move large quantities of data.

Another common Service Broker messaging pattern is the long-running conversation. Because Service Broker dialogs are persistent, a conversation between two endpoints can last for weeks or even years. A good example of a long-running conversation is the purchase order conversation between a book store and a publisher. The bookstore sends a purchase order to the publisher containing the list of books ordered. The publisher responds with prices and delivery dates. There might be a long exchange of messages reaching agreement on these items. The publisher then sends a series of status messages as the order is printed and shipped. When the shipment is received, the store acknowledges receipt and then there is an exchange of messages involved with payment, returns, quality control, etc. This conversation may last for several weeks and involve dozens of messages. Service Broker dialogs and conversation groups help manage this exchange of messages and maintain the current state of the order.

As part of designing the services for your application, you must decide which of these messaging patterns are most suitable for each service. Service Broker supports any combination of these patterns, so there are many options to choose from when designing message flows.

Dialog Lifetime

When designing messages and dialogs, you should also determine how long your dialogs should live. The dialog lifetime—set with the **LIFETIME** parameter of the **BEGIN DIALOG** command—can range from a few seconds to forever. Most dialogs last as long as the interaction they were created for. In many of the request-response dialogs shown in the samples in this book, the dialog is terminated after a single message has been sent in each direction. In such cases, the dialog lifetime should be set to a value at least several times as long as you would expect the dialog to take under normal circumstances. For example, if a typical message exchange takes 5 seconds, you may want to set the dialog lifetime to a minute or so.

You should keep in mind that when the dialog lifetime expires, the dialog will be forced into an error state and there is nothing you can do with the dialog except to end it. For this reason, if you want dialogs to last through network outages that may last several hours, you must set the **LIFETIME** parameter long enough to outlast the network outage. One of the more common errors I see in Service Broker applications is setting the **LIFETIME** parameter to too low a value, so the dialog expires before the application is done using it.

A related decision is whether to start a new dialog for every conversation or to reuse dialogs. Dialogs are pretty lightweight, but you may find that creating a new dialog for sending each message introduces an intolerable amount of overhead if the message volume is very high. In this case, it may make sense to reuse dialogs instead of throwing them away after each use. Reusing dialogs can reduce overhead, but you need to be careful, because dialogs impose a processing order on messages. For example, if you decide to create five dialogs and send messages in a round-robin fashion on these five dialogs, you will reduce the dialog startup and shutdown overhead, but you may severely limit performance. Only five messages will ever be processed in parallel, because processing each message holds a lock on the conversation group for the message. If you decide to reuse dialogs, be sure to design the ability to change the number of dialogs used into your application.

I have worked with several applications where the customer only wants to use a single dialog because they want all messages processed in order. To satisfy this requirement, I came up with a stored procedure that checks for the dialog in the database and only creates a new one if no dialogs exist for that service. In the application where this was used, messages were sent by an external application that connected to the database. This stored procedure remembers the dialog handle and passes it in when calling the stored procedure. When the application starts, it passes in a NULL for the dialog handle and the stored procedure returns the handle to use. Listing 13.1 shows a simplified version of the stored procedure.

```
CREATE PROCEDURE [dbo].[SendOnReusableDialog]

@Message varbinary(max),
@dialog1 UNIQUEIDENTIFIER OUTPUT -- in out
as

if @dialog1 is null
Begin
        select Top(1) @dialog1 = conversation_handle from
➲  sys.conversation_endpoints e
                join sys.services s on e.service_id = s.service_id
                where e.is_initiator = 1 and s.name = 'SingleDialogService'
```

```
        IF (@@ROWCOUNT = 0)
        Begin
                -- No useable dialog found so start a new one
                BEGIN DIALOG @dialog1
                        FROM SERVICE [SingleDialogService]
                        TO SERVICE 'SingleDialogTargetService'
                        ON CONTRACT [TestContract]
                WITH ENCRYPTION = OFF
        End
End

declare @tries int
set @tries = 0

-- Send the message
resend:

;SEND ON CONVERSATION @dialog1
        MESSAGE TYPE [TestMessage]
        (@Message)

declare @converror int
set @converror = @@error
if ((@converror = 8426 or @converror = 8429) and @tries < 3)
begin
        if (@converror = 8429) End conversation @dialog1
        -- The dialog passed in is no longer active so open a new one
        BEGIN DIALOG @dialog1
                FROM SERVICE [SingleDialogService]
                TO SERVICE 'SingleDialogTargetService'
                ON CONTRACT [TestContract]
                WITH ENCRYPTION = OFF
        if (@@error = 0)
```

```
     Begin

            set @tries = @tries + 1 -- increment a retry count so we don't
⊃loop forever

            goto resend

     end
end
```

Listing 13.1: Sending on a Reusable Dialog.

While you should make an effort to determine the proper dialog lifetime for each dialog you begin, after the application has been running a while, experience or changing conditions might tell you that you made the wrong decision. Be sure to design your application so that it is easy to change the lifetime if necessary.

Handling Responses and Errors

Almost all services will generate either response messages or errors back to the caller. Dealing with these messages is the final aspect of dialog design. How these are handled depends on the control flow of the application. If the application can't continue until it receives the results from the services it has called, then the main thread of execution of the application must wait for the results before continuing. The code for this type of operation would look like the parallel stored procedure code in Listing 12.1 in Chapter 12. The main thread sends out multiple messages to services that will be executed in parallel and then goes into a loop, waiting for all the responses to return before continuing. This isn't the most efficient application pattern, but in some cases it is necessary to satisfy the business requirements of an application that can't return until all required operations have completed. Using this pattern for invoking services only makes sense when several services can execute in parallel or if the service is a remote service.

The more efficient way to handle responses is to use a separate service to handle the responses and errors and do whatever processing is required. In many cases, the main thread of the application will have completed long before responses are received from some of the services it started. These services might communicate with the application by updating the state of the application. For example, when the order entry application receives a notification that the order has been shipped, the order status would be changed to "Shipped" and the shipment information would be added to the order. An activated stored procedure often works well for handling responses because messages will arrive at random times as the services complete. Listings 13.2 and 13.3 show the same application as Listing 12.1 in Chapter 12, split into the main application thread that sends messages to the service and an activated service linked to the response queue to handle response messages.

```
ALTER PROCEDURE AsyncOrder as

DECLARE @message XML
Set @message =
N'<?xml version="1.0"?><ShippingRequest
➲ xmlns="http://schemas.adventure-works.com/demo/ShippingRequest"
➲ xmlns:xsi="http://www.w3.org/2001/XMLSchema-instance" >
        <SalesOrderID>87362</SalesOrderID>
        <Customer>
                <fname>Larry</fname>
                <lname>Simpson</lname>
                <address11>One Microsoft Way</address11>
                <city>Redmond</city>
                <state>WA</state>
                <country>USA</country>
        </Customer>
        <ProductDetail>
                <productID>83662</productID>
                <quantity>3</quantity>
                <price>3.14</price>
        </ProductDetail>
        <ProductDetail>
                <productID>263745</productID>
                <quantity>2</quantity>
                <price>19.95</price>
        </ProductDetail>
</ShippingRequest>';

DECLARE @OrderID uniqueidentifier

-- Insert a record for this order into the state table. The order ID
-- is a GUID that will also be used as the conversation ID
```

```
SET @OrderID = NEWID()
Insert into OEState values (@OrderID, N'Initial', 0, 0, 0)

BEGIN TRANSACTION;
-- Start the three dialogs we will use to call the three services
-- Put all three in the same conversation group linked to the state table
⤴ key.
DECLARE @PODialog uniqueidentifier
BEGIN DIALOG @PODialog FROM SERVICE [OrderEntryService]
        TO SERVICE 'SOAPOService'  ON CONTRACT POContract
        WITH RELATED_CONVERSATION_GROUP = @OrderID;

DECLARE @InventoryDialog uniqueidentifier
BEGIN DIALOG @InventoryDialog FROM SERVICE [OrderEntryService]
        TO SERVICE 'SOAInventoryService'  ON CONTRACT InventoryContract
        WITH RELATED_CONVERSATION_GROUP = @OrderID;

DECLARE @CreditDialog uniqueidentifier
BEGIN DIALOG @CreditDialog FROM SERVICE [OrderEntryService]
        TO SERVICE 'SOACreditCheckService' ON CONTRACT CreditContract
        WITH RELATED_CONVERSATION_GROUP = @OrderID;

-- Send the messages to invoke the services for this order
SEND ON CONVERSATION @CreditDialog MESSAGE TYPE
⤴ [OrderMessage](@message);
SEND ON CONVERSATION @PODialog MESSAGE TYPE [OrderMessage](@message);
SEND ON CONVERSATION @InventoryDialog MESSAGE TYPE [OrderMessage] (@message);
-- Update the state to indicate that the messages have been sent
Update OEState SET Status = N'Messages Sent' WHERE OrderID = @OrderID
COMMIT
```

Listing 13.2: Sending Service Requests.

The procedure in Listing 13.3 is activated by messages arriving on the response queue and handles response and error messages.

```
ALTER PROCEDURE OrderResponse as

DECLARE @conversationHandle uniqueidentifier
declare @message_body nvarchar(MAX)
declare @message_type_name sysname;
declare @conversation_group_id uniqueidentifier;

while 1 = 1
begin
        -- Receive Response messages
        Begin Transaction
        WaitFor (
        RECEIVE top(1)
                @message_type_name=message_type_name,
                @conversationHandle=conversation_handle,
                @message_body=message_body,
                @conversation_group_id=conversation_group_id
                FROM OrderQueue
        ), Timeout 2000

        if @@rowcount = 0
        Begin
                rollback
                Break
        end
    .   -- Handle the return messages from the services. In reality there
➲would
        -- be a significant amount of logic here to deal with the various
➲conditions

        -- that could be returned
        if @message_type_name = N'CreditStatus'
                Begin
                        -- Update the state table to indicate the response has
➲been received
```

```
                              Update OEState SET CRDone = 1 WHERE OrderID =
⊃@conversation_group_id
                              END CONVERSATION @conversationHandle
               End
        if @message_type_name = N'InventoryStatus'
               Begin
                              Update OEState SET INVDone = 1 WHERE OrderID =
⊃@conversation_group_id
                              END CONVERSATION @conversationHandle
               End
        if @message_type_name = N'POInformation'
               Begin
                              Update OEState SET PODone = 1 WHERE OrderID =
⊃@conversation_group_id
                              END CONVERSATION @conversationHandle
               End
        -- When all the responses have been received, mark the order as
⊃complete
        Update OEState SET Status = N'All Messages Received' WHERE OrderID =
⊃@conversation_group_id
                      and INVDone = 1 and PODone = 1 and CRDone = 1
        Commit
End
```

Listing 13.3: Handling Asynchronous Responses.

Note that this example would have to be expanded to handle error messages returned from the service or from Service Broker and a variety of responses from each service.

Implementation

Now that we have discussed the important design decisions that must be made for a service-oriented application, let's spend a little time discussing implementation issues. This isn't a comprehensive guide to implementing Service Broker applications, but a brief overview of some of the issues you should consider.

For each service, you must decide whether it should be implemented as a TSQL stored procedure, a CLR stored procedure, or an external application. If the service primarily manipulates database data, a stored procedure will probably be the best implementation choice. If the service just uses data in the message to update the database, a TSQL stored procedure is best. If it does a significant amount of processing before updating the database—complex XML transformations, for example—a CLR stored procedure will be more efficient. If the service manipulates external data, devices, or networks, it should be implemented as an external application. Services that do a significant amount of processing and a minimal amount of database I\O should also be implemented as external applications. Remember that external applications can easily scale out by moving the processing to another server.

If you are modifying an existing application, you must also decide whether to modify the existing logic to create the new service, wrap the existing logic in a service wrapper, or implement a new service to replace the existing logic. You may also convert an existing application into a service by wrapping the executable with a service wrapper that receives messages, passes them to the application for processing, and converts the output of the application into return messages. This is often a good strategy for getting a service-oriented application running and then refining it by rewriting the external executables as services over a period of time.

Whenever I work with developers on writing Service Broker applications, I recommend implementing the Service Broker infrastructure—messages, services, queues, routes, and so on—before starting to implement the service code itself. The actual services can be simulated by simple stored procedures that receive and send "canned" messages. Once the basic infrastructure is working the way you designed it, you can replace the dummy services with the real ones, one at a time. This process is especially important for the first couple of service-oriented applications you implement. If the underlying infrastructure is working correctly, it is easier to debug issues with the services.

As you are developing services, use the SQL Server trace facilities to monitor the Service Broker background processes that are handling the messages. Some issues (like dropped messages or multiple retries being necessary to deliver a message) aren't visible except through traces.

Deployment

If you kept the dummy scripts you wrote to simulate services during development, deployment is a good time to drag them out again. Set up the Service Broker infrastructure, make sure the right messages are going to all the right places, and use traces to ensure everything is working the way it should. Once the infrastructure is operating correctly, take the time to thoroughly document all the Service Broker metadata required to set it up. Put all the scripts under source control so that you can recreate the setup when necessary. Set up reminders so that you will be informed a few weeks before the expiration of any certificates that you created. Be sure you are monitoring the file groups where queues are located, so that you know when they are running low on space. Set up event notifications for poison messages on all the queues that your application uses. See Chapter 8 for a review of poison message handling.

Once you are sure your infrastructure is working correctly, start installing the real services one at a time and testing after each installation. Run a full set of functional tests and then do stress testing on the target environment, so that you know how your application reacts to extreme load conditions. Test failover and make sure all procedures for handling failures are well documented. As with any new system, you should run side by side with the old system for a while and compare results to make sure there are no surprises when you go live. Before going live, check all the queues for messages left over from testing and make sure there are no extraneous dialogs in any of the **sys.conversation_endpoints** tables. If you want to ensure the whole database is set back to its original state, you can use the following command:

```
ALTER DATABASE myDB SET NEW_BROKER
```

 Caution:

This command will get rid of all conversations and queued messages. This is a drastic measure, so make sure you really want to get rid of all Service Broker messages and dialogs in the database before you use it. After they're gone isn't a good time to remember that there were a bunch of important messages from another application in the database.

Once the application is up and running, continue to monitor it for dropped messages, queues filling up, excessive retries, and so on, until you are confident that it is working the way you want. You should practice fault recovery occasionally to make sure everyone knows what to do when services fail.

Servicing

One of the often overlooked advantages of service-oriented applications is that fixing, upgrading and replacing services is almost trivially easy. You can set up a new service next to the existing one and let it process some of the messages from the queue to make sure it works correctly with live data. Once it is running to your satisfaction, you just shut down the old service, and you'll be running on the new service with no interruption in service. This works even if you are replacing a wrapped COBOL program with a brand new C# stored procedure. Even if you decide to shut down the service while making the changeover, reliable Service Broker messaging will ensure that no messages are lost. By replacing one service at a time, you can gradually replace a whole application with no application downtime.

Summary

Service-Oriented Architecture offers many advantages in application flexibility, performance, distribution, and reuse. Basing your service-oriented application on the Service Broker infrastructure adds reliability and fault tolerance to this architectural approach. Service Broker also simplifies the design, construction, deployment, and servicing of service-oriented applications.

Did you know?

SOA is a very over-used acronym. A quick Web search turned up the following examples:

- Steadicam Operators Association
- Start Of Authority
- Society Of Actuaries
- Supervisor of Assessments
- Special Operations Association
- Semiconductor Organic Analyzer
- Shipwrecks of Anatolia

Chapter 14

Scheduling with Service Broker

All the talk about service-oriented applications in Chapter 13 might have given you the impression that Service Broker is just an application development infrastructure, and that if you're not building a new application, Service Broker wouldn't be relevant. In reality, Service Broker is a great way to perform a variety of asynchronous database tasks that have nothing to do application development. I expect many DBAs will find Service Broker an invaluable tool for scheduling and managing SQL Server jobs.

Using Activation and Conversations to Start Jobs

Let's review a bit. Activation is a Service Broker feature that will start a user-defined stored procedure to receive and process messages that arrive on a queue. A Service Broker conversation ensures that messages in the same dialog are processed in the order they were sent. One definition of batch processing is starting a series of SQL statements in a defined order. Putting all this together, we find that an activated stored procedure that receives messages containing SQL statements and executes them in dialog order fits the definition of a SQL batch processor. (In this case, "batch" is a generic term for a group of jobs, rather than the specific concept of a SQL Server batch).

This section shows you examples of how to use Service Broker to implement a simple batch execution system. Each batch will be a dialog containing one message for each SQL statement you wish to run. Because these messages are contained in a dialog, they will be executed in order. Because the messages are received in a transaction and the queue and dialog are persistent, the batch will survive any hardware failures and database restarts.

Dialogs and conversation group locking ensure that messages are processed one after another and a job won't start until the previous one completes. If a job fails, you can use the **END CONVERSATION** statement to cancel the batch, so that no statements after the failed statement will execute.

The following example shows how to set up a batch processing system that uses Service Broker. The script in Listing 14.1 just sets up the Service Broker objects that the batch processor will use.

```
CREATE DATABASE BatchProcessingDB
go
USE BatchProcessingDBgo
-- Create the message type for the Jobs we are going to queue
CREATE MESSAGE TYPE [JobRequest] VALIDATION = NONE
CREATE MESSAGE TYPE [EndBatch] VALIDATION = NONE

-- Create the message type for Job response messages that indicate that the
⊃Job has succeeded
CREATE MESSAGE TYPE [JobStatusResponse] VALIDATION = NONE
CREATE CONTRACT [JobsContract]
        ([JobRequest] SENT BY initiator,
         [EndBatch] SENT BY initiator,
         [JobStatusResponse] SENT BY target);
-- Create the queues we're going to use
CREATE QUEUE [JobQueue]
CREATE QUEUE [JobStatusQueue]
Go
-- Create the Services.  Services are essentially aliases for queues
CREATE SERVICE [JobRequestService] ON QUEUE [JobQueue]
        (
        [JobsContract]
        );
CREATE SERVICE [JobStatusResponseService] ON QUEUE [JobStatusQueue]
```

Listing 14.1: Service Broker Objects for Batch Processing.

The script in Listing 14.2 creates a stored procedure that receives messages, extracts a SQL statement from the message body, executes the statement, and returns the result to the dialog initiator.

```
CREATE PROCEDURE [dbo].[ProcessStatementsProc]
AS
DECLARE          @message_type_name sysname
DECLARE          @dialog uniqueidentifier
DECLARE          @message_body xml
DECLARE          @BatchNumber bigint
DECLARE          @StatementNumber bigint
DECLARE          @Command nvarchar(3000)
DECLARE          @NoTransaction int
DECLARE          @ErrorNumber bigint
DECLARE          @ErrorText nvarchar(MAX)
DECLARE          @MsgSequence bigint
DECLARE          @MsgSequenceOrig bigint

WHILE (1 = 1)
BEGIN
        BEGIN TRANSACTION


-- Receive the next available message
        WAITFOR (
                RECEIVE top(1)
                        @message_type_name=message_type_name,
                        @message_body=message_body,
                        @MsgSequenceOrig = message_sequence_number,
                        @dialog = conversation_handle
                        FROM [JobQueue]
        ), TIMEOUT 5000
        IF (@@ROWCOUNT = 0)
                BEGIN
                        ROLLBACK TRANSACTION
                        BREAK
                END
```

```
    -- Handle the End Conversation Message
        IF (@message_type_name =
'http://schemas.microsoft.com/SQL/ServiceBroker/EndDialog')
        BEGIN
                -- When we receive an End Dialog, we need to end also.
                END CONVERSATION @dialog
        END
        ELSE
    -- Handle the Conversation Error Message
        IF (@message_type_name =
'http://schemas.microsoft.com/SQL/ServiceBroker/Error')
        BEGIN
                -- We can't return anything here because the dialog at the
other end is closed so just log an error and
                -- close our end of the conversation.
                END CONVERSATION @dialog
        END
        ELSE
        IF (@message_type_name = 'JobRequest')
        -- Process normal Job messages.  You could easily
        -- define multiple message types to represent different
        -- types of Jobs.
        BEGIN

                -- Pull the information out of the Job message
                SELECT @BatchNumber =
@message_body.value('(/Job/BatchNumber)[1]', 'bigint'),
                    @StatementNumber =
@message_body.value('(/Job/StatementNumber)[1]', 'bigint'),
                    @NoTransaction =
@message_body.value('(/Job/NoTransaction)[1]', 'int'),
                    @Command = @message_body.value('(/Job/Command)[1]',
'nvarchar(3000)')

                SELECT  @ErrorNumber = 0, @ErrorText = N''
                -- We can't have a transaction active for a backup
```

```
IF (@NoTransaction = 1) COMMIT
-- Execute the command
BEGIN TRY
EXEC (@Command)
END TRY
BEGIN CATCH
SELECT @ErrorNumber = error_number(),
       @ErrorText = error_message()
-- Get rid of the bad message
IF (@NoTransaction <> 1)
BEGIN
        ROLLBACK TRANSACTION
        BEGIN TRANSACTION ;
        RECEIVE top(1)
            @MsgSequence = message_sequence_number
            FROM [JobQueue]
            WHERE conversation_handle = @dialog
        IF (@MsgSequence <> @MsgSequenceOrig)
        BEGIN
            -- Another thread already got the message
            ROLLBACK
            BEGIN TRANSACTION
        END
END
END CATCH

IF (@NoTransaction = 1) BEGIN TRANSACTION
-- Send a response message saying we're done
DECLARE @ResponseDoc xml
DECLARE @Time nvarchar(100)
SET @Time = cast(getdate() as nvarchar(100))

-- Fill in the XML document with job information.
SET @ResponseDoc = N'<JobStatus/>'
SET @ResponseDoc.modify(
```

```
'insert (<BatchNumber>{ sql:variable("@BatchNumber") }</BatchNumber>,
⤶<StatementNumber>{ sql:variable("@StatementNumber")
⤶}</StatementNumber>,
<ErrorNumber>{ sql:variable("@ErrorNumber") }</ErrorNumber>,
<ErrorText>{ sql:variable("@ErrorText") }</ErrorText>,
<Time>{ sql:variable("@Time") }</Time>
) as last into (/JobStatus)[1]');

                    SEND ON CONVERSATION @dialog
                        MESSAGE TYPE [JobStatusResponse] (@ResponseDoc)

                -- Optionally, if the Job failed, you may want to execute:
                -- END CONVERSATION @dialog WITH
                --      ERROR = @ErrorNumber DESCRIPTION = @ErrorText
                -- to prevent other dependant Jobs from executing
            END -- process Job
            -- If this is the last job in the batch, End the Conversation.
            IF (@message_type_name = 'EndBatch')
            BEGIN
                    END CONVERSATION @dialog
            END

            COMMIT TRANSACTION
END -- while loop
```

Listing 14.2: Batch Execution Stored Procedure.

By now, the first part of this stored procedure should look very familiar—it's the same message loop used in almost all the samples thus far. The interesting part starts with: IF(@message_type_name = 'JobRequest'). This is the handling code for JobRequest messages. This handling logic starts by extracting the job information from the XML document in the **message_body** with XQuery. Next, the SQL command is executed with an **EXEC** statement in a **TRY ... CATCH** block. If an error is caught, we save off the error information, roll back the transaction, and then receive the message again to make sure we get it off the queue. Notice that we check the sequence number against the original sequence number for the message to make sure we got the right one. It's possible that another thread got to the message first, so if the sequence numbers don't match, we roll back the receive transaction so that the message can be received again. Next, the information about the job is assembled into an XML document and sent back to the initiator queue. Receiving and committing the message takes it off the queue so the dialog continues with the next message. In some cases, the right behavior would be to call **END CONVERSATION** to terminate the batch. Which approach you choose depends on the semantics of your application.

In a real application, you would want to do more work on error detection and return more detailed information about each statement that executes, but this brief sample should get you started. To use this procedure, set it up as an activated procedure for the **JobQueue** using the following statement. Notice that the **MAX_QUEUE_READERS** parameter can be used to control how many jobs will execute in parallel.

```
ALTER QUEUE [JobQueue] WITH ACTIVATION ( STATUS = ON,
    PROCEDURE_NAME = ProcessStatementsProc ,
    MAX_QUEUE_READERS = 4, EXECUTE AS SELF );
```

Now that we have a stored procedure that will process jobs that are sent as Service Broker messages, we need to set up a procedure to handle the return messages. To keep things simple, this example stores the returned status in a table. The statement in Listing 14.3 creates the table that stores job status.

```
CREATE TABLE JobStatus (
        BatchNumber bigint ,
        StatementNumber bigint
           primary key(BatchNumber, StatementNumber),
        ProcessStatus   int null,
        EndTime         datetime null,

        ErrorXML XML null )
```

Listing 14.3: Job Status Table.

The script in Listing 14.4 creates a stored procedure that receives status messages and logs them to the **JobStatus** table.

```
CREATE PROCEDURE [dbo].[HandleJobStatus] AS

declare         @message_type_name sysname
declare         @dialog uniqueidentifier
declare         @message_body XML

while (1 = 1)
begin
        begin transaction
        WAITFOR (
                RECEIVE top(1)
                        @message_type_name=message_type_name,
                        @message_body=message_body,
                        @dialog = conversation_handle
                        FROM [JobStatusQueue]
        ), TIMEOUT 5000
        if (@@ROWCOUNT = 0)
                BEGIN
                        ROLLBACK TRANSACTION
                        BREAK
                END
        IF (@message_type_name =
➲'http://schemas.microsoft.com/SQL/ServiceBroker/EndDialog')
        BEGIN
                End Conversation @dialog
        END
        ELSE
        IF (@message_type_name =
➲'http://schemas.microsoft.com/SQL/ServiceBroker/Error')
        BEGIN
                -- Write the error to a log table
                -- End the dialog
                End Conversation @dialog
        END
        ELSE
        IF (@message_type_name = 'JobStatusResponse')
```

```
        BEGIN

                -- Insert the XML status data into the status table
                INSERT INTO JobStatus (BatchNumber, StatementNumber,
                        ProcessStatus, EndTime, ErrorXML)
                    VALUES (
    @message_body.value('(/JobStatus/BatchNumber)[1]', 'bigint'),
    @message_body.value('(/JobStatus/StatementNumber)[1]', 'bigint'),
    @message_body.value('(/JobStatus/ErrorNumber)[1]', 'bigint'),
    @message_body.value('(/JobStatus/Time)[1]','nvarchar(100)'),
    @message_body)


        END -- process Task status
        COMMIT TRANSACTION
END -- while loop
go
ALTER QUEUE [JobStatusQueue]
        WITH ACTIVATION (
                STATUS = ON,
                PROCEDURE_NAME = [HandleJobStatus],
                MAX_QUEUE_READERS = 1,
                EXECUTE AS SELF
        )
```

Listing 14.4: Handling Return Messages.

The procedure in Listing 14.4 receives messages, and if the message is a 'JobStatusResponse' message, the message_body is parsed and the information is inserted into the **JobStatus** table. The more observant among you are probably asking why not just insert the status into the table in the **ProcessStatementsProc** procedure? While this certainly could be done, I used the more general case for this example. Since messages are sent back to the initiator, this sample could be used to initiate jobs on many different databases from a common administrative database that tracks the status of all jobs.

The next step in this sample is to send some jobs to be executed by the batch processing system. The script in Listing 14.5 will send two batches—one that creates and then drops a table, and a second one that backs up a non-existent database. I chose to back up a non-existent database to demonstrate error handling, but you obviously can change this to a real database. Since everything happens in the background, you will have to look at the **JobStatus** table to see what happened. If there aren't any records there, look in the SQL Server error log for output from the stored procedures.

```
DECLARE @msgbody XML
DECLARE          @conversationHandle uniqueidentifier

BEGIN DIALOG CONVERSATION @conversationHandle
        FROM SERVICE    [JobStatusResponseService]
        TO SERVICE      'JobRequestService'
        ON CONTRACT     [JobsContract]

SET @msgbody = N'
<Job>
  <BatchNumber>1</BatchNumber>
  <StatementNumber>20</StatementNumber>
  <Command>CREATE TABLE Account (Col1 int primary key, Col2 int)</Command>
  <NoTransaction>0</NoTransaction>
</Job>';
SEND ON CONVERSATION @conversationHandle
        MESSAGE TYPE [JobRequest] (@msgbody);

SET @msgbody = N'
<Job>
  <BatchNumber>1</BatchNumber>
  <StatementNumber>10</StatementNumber>
  <Command>DROP TABLE Account</Command>
  <NoTransaction>0</NoTransaction>
</Job>';
SEND ON CONVERSATION @conversationHandle
        MESSAGE TYPE [JobRequest] (@msgbody);
```

```
SEND ON CONVERSATION @conversationHandle
        MESSAGE TYPE [EndBatch] (' ');

BEGIN DIALOG CONVERSATION @conversationHandle
        FROM SERVICE    [JobStatusResponseService]
        TO SERVICE      'JobRequestService'
        ON CONTRACT     [JobsContract]

SET @msgbody = N'
<Job>
  <BatchNumber>5</BatchNumber>
  <StatementNumber>10</StatementNumber>
  <Command>BACKUP DATABASE PayablesDB TO DISK = ''c:\PayablesDB.bak'' WITH INIT
➲</Command>
  <NoTransaction>1</NoTransaction>
</Job>';
SEND ON CONVERSATION @conversationHandle
        MESSAGE TYPE [JobRequest] (@msgbody);
SEND ON CONVERSATION @conversationHandle
        MESSAGE TYPE [EndBatch] (' ');
```

Listing 14.5: Queuing Sample Jobs.

Notice that the two batches are sent on different dialogs. This means that the two batches can execute in parallel. All the jobs in a single batch execute one after the other to preserve order. If your jobs don't need to execute in order, they should be put into different dialogs so they can execute in parallel if possible.

Scheduling with Conversation Timers

In addition to controlling batch execution and managing activation and parallelism, Service Broker offers conversation timers, which are great for scheduling tasks. A conversation timer puts a message on a queue after a user-defined delay. Like any Service Broker message, a conversation timer message can activate a stored procedure, so a conversation timer can be used to execute a SQL statement at some time in the future. The advantage of using conversation timers is that they are persistent timers. This means that once a timer has started, you can be sure it will fire in spite of power failures, disaster failovers, and even moving the database to another server.

The logic to create a scheduled job using conversation timers is very simple. The example in Listing 14.6 demonstrates how to create a task that will do a log backup once a minute.

```
-- Set up a queue for the timer sample
CREATE QUEUE [TimerQueue]
CREATE SERVICE [TimerService] ON QUEUE [TimerQueue]([DEFAULT]) ;
CREATE SERVICE [TimerResponseService] ON QUEUE [TimerQueue];
GO


-- Create the stored procedure to handle the timer messages
CREATE PROCEDURE [dbo].[HandleTimer] AS

        DECLARE         @conversationHandle uniqueidentifier
        DECLARE         @message_type_name sysname
        DECLARE         @dialog uniqueidentifier
        BEGIN TRANSACTION
        -- Timer messages only happen once a minute so there's no
        -- need to receive in a loop.
        WAITFOR (
                RECEIVE top(1)
                        @message_type_name=message_type_name,
                        @dialog = conversation_handle
                        FROM [TimerQueue]
        ), TIMEOUT 500
        IF (@message_type_name =
⊃'http://schemas.microsoft.com/SQL/ServiceBroker/DialogTimer')
        BEGIN
                -- Start the next cycle
                BEGIN CONVERSATION TIMER ( @dialog ) TIMEOUT = 60;
                -- Must commit here because backup doesn't work
                --in a transaction
                COMMIT TRANSACTION
                BACKUP LOG ShippingDB TO DISK = 'c:\ShippingDB.bak'
```

```
                WITH INIT
      END
      ELSE
            -- Just ignore other message types
            COMMIT TRANSACTION
go
ALTER QUEUE [TimerQueue] WITH ACTIVATION (
            STATUS = ON, PROCEDURE_NAME = HandleTimer ,
            MAX_QUEUE_READERS = 1,EXECUTE AS SELF)
```

Listing 14.6: Scheduling with Conversation Timer.

The sample starts by creating a queue and services for the conversation timers to use. Notice that the initiator and target are on the same queue. Normally I wouldn't recommend this, because listening to both ends of the conversation at once is the Service Broker equivalent of talking to yourself. In this application, however, no messages are sent to the target, so there shouldn't be any confusion. The procedure to handle the timer messages receives a message, and if the message type is DialogTimer, it backs up the log and starts the timer for the next backup. This procedure is one of the few cases where I don't recommend using a receive loop, because the messages only come once a minute. It makes sense to let Service Broker Activation start a new stored procedure for every message.

The other thing to note is that this procedure starts the conversation timer and commits the transaction before calling the backup statement. Normally, you should execute the statement and then reset the timer so that the time is measured from the end of the statement. For this example, the process is reversed because a backup statement can't be executed in a transaction. Resetting the timer before committing the transaction ensures that the timer will start, even if the system goes down during the backup. There is a little risk here because if a log backup takes more than a minute, two of them will be running at once. You should make certain the timeout is long enough to ensure that there won't be an overlap.

The conversation timer is a persistent, transactional timer. It will keep doing backups until the dialog is manually terminated. If the database is stopped and restarted later, the backups will start again as soon as the database starts again. The timer doesn't get reset while the database isn't running, so you won't have to deal with 30 backups starting simultaneously when the database is restarted after being down for a half hour (the way old Unix **cron** jobs used to). Any timers that expired while the database was down will fire as soon as the database is restarted. If you have a lot of different timers running, you could have a great deal of activity right after restarting the database. Because the timer is part of the database, if the database is moved to another server, the timer moves with it and the backups will continue.

Now that we have the conversation timer handling set up, we just have to start the first one to get the cycle started. Run the script in Listing 14.7 to test the procedure.

```
DECLARE @conversationHandle uniqueidentifier
BEGIN DIALOG CONVERSATION @conversationHandle
        FROM SERVICE     [TimerResponseService]
        TO SERVICE       'TimerService';
BEGIN CONVERSATION TIMER ( @ConversationHandle ) TIMEOUT = 60;
```

Listing 14.7: Starting the Conversation Timer.

Notice that the dialog is started without a lifetime, so that it will keep running forever. The easiest way to kill the timer is to look up the conversation handle with a statement like this:

```
SELECT conversation_handle FROM sys.conversation_endpoints
     WHERE far_service = 'TimerService'
```

Use the **conversation_handle** value to end the conversation.

Now that you know the basics, you can use them to build as sophisticated a scheduling system as you require. For example, you could create a table that has columns for the conversation handle, the time interval, and the statement to run when the timer expires. When the stored procedure receives a DialogTimer message, it would use the **conversation_ handle** column from the message to look up the statement to run and the time interval in the table, execute the statement, and reset the timer to the time interval retrieved. This simple expansion of the example would support a number of jobs being scheduled from the same queue. The timer table could also store the status of the last time the statement executed and a flag to tell the procedure to end the dialog instead of resetting the timer the next time a message is received. If you want to schedule a job to run at a particular time instead of periodically, just set the timer to fire after the required time and don't reset the conversation timer when it expires.

Summary

In addition to being a great asynchronous database development platform, Service Broker can be a job scheduling and execution system. A typical system has dozens of jobs and batches of jobs that must be run periodically to keep the database running well and populated with current data. Typical examples are backups, index rebuilds, data warehouse load jobs, and data extraction. The distributed nature of the Service Broker supports batch execution and scheduling for any number of databases distributed through the network.

FREE

Bonus:

The following bonus material is available for free downloading when you register your book at www.rationalpress.com **(see the last page in this book for instructions):**

▶   **Sample code for the examples in this book**

▶   **Bonus Chapter: "Troubleshooting and Administration"**

Did you know?

While it is turned off by default for security reasons, using xp_cmdshell would allow you to schedule Windows jobs using Service Broker.

Extras

Glossary

Activation	Starting the correct number of stored procedures to handle the number of incoming messages on a queue. If a stored procedure is associated with a queue, Service Broker will start a copy of the stored procedure when the first message arrives on the queue and then start additional copies if the current number of stored procedures is unable to keep up with the incoming rate.
Adjacent Broker Protocol	A TCP/IP based protocol used to transfer Service Broker messages between two database instances through a network connection.
AES	Advanced Encryption Algorithm. An advanced, highly secure symmetric key encryption algorithm. One of two algorithms supported by Service Broker Adjacent Broker connections.
Anonymous Conversation	An anonymous conversation is only authenticated in one direction. The initiator of the conversation knows the identity of the target but the target doesn't know the identity of the initiator. This is useful when hundreds or thousands of initiators connect to the same target. If they connect anonymously, the target doesn't have to maintain certificates to authenticate all the initiators.
Asymmetric Encryption	Asymmetric encryption uses a pair of keys to encrypt and decrypt data. The asymmetric key pair consists of a public key and a private key. Data encrypted with the public key can only be decrypted by the private key. Data encrypted by the private key can only be decrypted by the public key.

Asynchronous Operation	A process calls an asynchronous operation by starting the operation and then going on to do other things while the asynchronous operation completes. The caller doesn't know exactly when the asynchronous operation starts or completes.
Authentication	A process by which a user's identity is reliably established by a system or application. Windows authentication uses passwords to prove identity. Service Broker uses either Windows authentication or certificates to establish the identity of users sending or receiving messages.
Authorization	Authorization determines what a particular user is allowed to do based on a configured set of permissions. In SQL Server, the **GRANT, DENY,** and **REVOKE** commands are used to set up authorization policies for a database.
BROKER_ INSTANCE	Parameter that indicates a particular Service Broker instance in a route or **BEGIN DIALOG** command. The parameter is a uniqueidentifier that matches the **service_broker_guid** column value in the sys.databases view.
Certificate	A standardized data structure containing an asymmetric key and other information that can be used to identify the owner of the certificate.
Contract	A SQL Server metadata object used to define which message types can be sent on a dialog and which dialog endpoint is allowed to send each message type.
Conversation	A reliable, bidirectional, ordered exchange of messages.

Conversation Group	All conversations are members of a conversation group. By default, each conversation is in its own conversation group, but an application may group related conversations together in a conversation group. When a message is received from a queue, all conversations in the same conversation group are locked for the duration of the transaction.
Conversation Timer	A feature of Service Broker conversations. A conversation timer is started with a time interval specified in seconds. When the timer expires, a message is placed on the queue for the service that started the timer.
Database Mirroring	A new feature of SQL Server 2005 that supports a backup copy of a database that is kept synchronized with the primary copy by sending altered database pages to the secondary copy and applying the changes.
Dequeue	Removing a message from a queue.
Dialog	A conversation between exactly two endpoints.
Endpoint	One of the termination points of a network connection. Service Broker defines two kinds of endpoints. A conversation endpoint is the source or destination of a conversation. Each conversation endpoint is associated with a queue. A Service Broker endpoint is one of several types of SQL Server endpoints which are connections to the network. Creating a Service Broker endpoint enables Service Broker communication over a TCP/IP network connection.
Enqueue	Putting a message on a queue. With Service Broker, this is an insert into the queue's hidden table.
Execute As	An activation parameter that specifies a user for the activated procedure to run as.

External Activation	Starting an external application to receive Service Broker messages. Service Broker doesn't currently include an external activation feature, but it provides hooks for external activation and a sample implementation.
Failover	The process of moving application processing to a standby system or database. Fault-tolerant systems generally have duplicate resources, so that if one system fails, another one can take over in a very short time.
KEK	Key Exchange Key. A symmetric key used to securely transfer session keys between Service Brokers. The KEK is exchanged between Service Brokers using highly-secure asymmetric key encryption and then the KEK is used to transfer the session keys used for each conversation. This means that expensive asymmetric key encryption is only used occasionally when the KEK must be replaced—not for every conversation.
KERBEROS	A network authentication protocol developed by MIT to provide strong identity verification across a variety of networks and platforms.
Loose Coupling	Coupling is a measure of how much of the internal working of a function or service the caller must know in order to successfully call it. In a loosely coupled system, the caller only has to understand the format and contents of a message that is sent to the service. The caller has no knowledge of the internal workings of the service it is calling.
Message Type	A SQL Server metadata object that assigns a name to a message. Optionally, a message type may define XML validation for the message contents.

msdb	One of the system databases created when SQL Server is installed. Service Broker uses routes stored in the msdb **sys. routes** table to route messages coming into a SQL Server instance.
NTLM	A proprietary Windows protocol used to authenticate a connection between two Windows processes over a network.
Peek	An operation provided by some messaging systems to allow you to see what messages are on a queue without receiving them. A peek is more lightweight than a receive operation because it doesn't lock or delete the message. The Service Broker equivalent is to do a select from the view built on the queue.
Profiler	A SQL Server tool that displays trace messages. Important for troubleshooting and monitoring Service Broker applications.
Queue	A temporary storage place for Service Broker messages. A Service Broker queue is implemented as a hidden SQL Server table. There are two types of queues: a user-defined queue that an application can receive messages from, and a transmission queue, which is an internal Service Broker object that holds messages temporarily while they are in route to their final destination.
Queue Reader	A process, stored procedure, or external program that receives messages from a queue.
RC4	An encryption algorithm for encrypting streams of data with a symmetric key. Developed by RSA Data Security. Generally, it is more efficient than the AES algorithm. RC4 and AES are the two encryption algorithms used to encrypt Service Broker data. RC4 is the default algorithm.
Remote Service Binding	A Service Broker metadata object used to associate a user with a remote service. The certificates this user owns are used to establish an authenticated conversation with a remote service.

Retention

A Service Broker queue parameter that causes the queue to save all the messages sent or received by services associated with the queue, until the dialog that owns the messages ends.

SChannel

The libraries necessary to implement an SSL connection between Windows applications are contained in the schannel.dll file.

Schema Collection

One or more schemas that will be used to validate the contents of an XML message. If there is more than one schema in the schema collection, the schema that defines the namespace used in the XML message body is used to validate the message.

Service

A Service Broker service is a name for a specific task or set of tasks that process Service Broker messages. Service Broker uses the name of the service to route messages, deliver messages to the correct queue within a database, and define security for a conversation. A service includes the queue where messages for this service are enqueued and a list of contracts that define the message types that the service handles.

Service Program

A program, stored procedure, or external application that sends and/or receives Service Broker messages.

Session Key

A symmetric key used to encrypt and sign Service Broker messages in a particular conversation. A session key is used by only one conversation.

SOA

Service-Oriented Architecture. An application architecture consisting of loosely coupled services hooked together with messaging.

SSL

Secure Sockets Layer. An encryption protocol developed by Netscape, used to transfer data privately and securely over a network.

State	Information that an application maintains between messages so that it can pick up processing from where it left off.
Symmetric Encryption	Also called "shared secret" encryption. A single key is used to encrypt and decrypt data. If two processes both have a copy of a symmetric key, they can securely exchange data between themselves. Symmetric encryption is much more efficient than asymmetric encryption.
Transactional Messaging	In a transactional messaging system, all send and receive operations take place in a transaction. If the transaction is rolled back, received messages are put back on the queue and sent messages are not sent. Transactional messaging applications are generally simpler to write and more robust in the face of failures.
Transmission Queue	A queue that temporarily holds messages that are being transferred between Service Broker services. For example, messages that are being sent from one Service Broker to another sit on the transmission queue until they have been successfully delivered to the remote Service Broker and an acknowledgement message has been received. Note that the acknowledgement message is handled by SQL Server, and is not visible to an application that uses Service Broker.
URL	Uniform Resource Locator. A standard label for a resource on a network. Most Service Broker names for global objects use the URL format to ensure uniqueness.
Validation	Checks the contents of a message body to ensure that its structure and contents conform to a particular XML schema.
VPN	Virtual Private Network. Uses encryption and other security techniques to establish a secure network connection through an unsecured network such as the Internet.

WAITFOR A SQL command that can wrap a Service Broker **RECEIVE** statement. A **RECEIVE** statement normally returns with 0 or more messages from the queue. If the **RECEIVE** statement is wrapped in a **WAITFOR** statement, it doesn't return until either a message is available on the queue or the **WAITFOR** timeout has expired.

Index

Notes

Notes

IMPORTANT NOTICE
REGISTER YOUR BOOK

Bonus Materials

Your book refers to valuable material that complements your learning experience. In order to download these materials you will need to register your book at http://www.rationalpress.com.

This bonus material is available after registration:

▶ Sample code for the examples in this book

▶ Bonus chapter: "Troubleshooting and Administration"

Registering your book

To register your book follow these 7 easy steps:

1. Go to http://www.rationalpress.com.

2. Create an account and login.

3. Click the **My Books** link.

4. Click the **Register New Book** button.

5. Enter the registration number found on the back of the book (Figure A).

6. Confirm registration and view your new book on the virtual bookshelf.

7. Click the spine of the desired book to view the available downloads and resources for the selected book.

Figure A: Back of your book.